Attic Kylix, 6th Cent. B.C. *(Courtesy Director of Antiquities, Cyprus Museum)*

PAPHOS
LAND OF APHRODITE

Written by
RENOS G. LAVITHIS

INTERWORLD PUBLICATIONS

PAPHOS
Land of Aphrodite

A South Western Cyprus Tourist Guide

Publisher: Renos Lavithis

Published by
INTERWORLD PUBLICATIONS
Member of Tophill Advertising and Promotions Ltd.
12 The Fairway, New Barnet
Herts. EN5 1HN, — England
Tel: 081-449 5938
Fax: 081-447 0599

CYPRUS AGENTS
14-16 King Constantine 12th Avenue
Paphos — Tel. 235056
Paphos — Tel. 237697

— First Published in 1983
— Second Revised Edition 1984
• Reprint in 1986
— Third Revised Edition 1987
• Reprint in 1989
— Fourth Revised Edition 1990
Reprint 1991

New Edition — 1992

Printed in Cyprus by PRINTCO LTD.

ISBN 0 948853 17 4

NOTICE
Every precaution has been taken to ensure accuracy of the information
contained in this book but the publishers accept no responsibility for
errors or omissions nor for statements in advertisements.

We will be very pleased to hear from our readers of comments, further
interesting information and personal observations.

All photographs (except those credited individually) have been taken by the author
– No reproduction is allowed.

CONTENTS

FOREWORD FROM THE AUTHOR

Paphos is alive again. After many hundreds of years of neglect and isolation, it is now fully revitalised with visitors from all over Europe.

This time you are not coming to pay homage to Aphrodite and participate in the annual celebrations; you are coming to admire the past, to enjoy the present and explore the beautiful and contrasting coast and countryside.

When as a youngster I used to wander around the empty spaces of Kato Paphos pretending to be an amateur archaeologist and sitting for hours watching the few barges loading carobs or almonds onto a lonely boat offshore, or unloading other goods, never did I imagine that the place, one day, would be buzzing with life, with an International Airport, only four hours away from London. Now the barges have gone and no commercial boats call to Paphos, but the small idyllic harbour is full of activity with fishing boats and pleasure boats.

This sudden and rapid expansion is good up to a point and I hope that the wisdom which prevailed so far will continue to restrict unscrupulous property developments, although, I must admit some isolated but very bad decisions were taken recently.

The first edition was produced in 1983 (64 pages). Then followed various re-prints and enlarged revised editions. Now the time has come for a new, enlarged book to cater for the ever changing face of Paphos which continues to evolve even at the time of going to press.

My biggest problem was to select the pictures out of a very large collection. I hope that the balance between photos and textual information provides a good picture of Paphos, to your satisfaction and pleasure. Enjoy the warmth of Paphos and I wish you a wonderful time.

Renos G. Lavithis.

ACKNOWLEDGEMENTS

Here I would like to express my heartfelt thanks to the following:

My wife Anna for all her encouragement, assisting me during our trips to various parts of Paphos, and her valuable contribution with the editing. My friend Dr. Stavros Panteli for all his help; Mr. Michael Mavroudis, who first originated the idea of this publication. Professor George Eliades who provided some useful information; Mr. Karlis Agrotis who assisted in the early stages driving me to many isolated places; to Dr. Demetris Michaelides archaeologist for his enormous contribution. The directors and staff of the Cyprus Museum and Cyprus Tourism Organisation; Mr. Stephanos Theodorou, Mr. Costas Kyriakou, Dr. C. Theophanides, Mr. Fivos Roussis, Mr. Elpi Paskalis; Petros Chiotis and Savvas Matsas with whom I explored the beauties of Akamas; David Pearlman, American archaeologist, who contributed so much to Paphos; Professor David Rupp of Ontario University; my friend Phytos and the numerous other individuals and organisations.

This book is dedicated to my daughter Niki K. Lavithis

CHAPTER 1

THE HISTORY OF PAPHOS

State of Paphos *(Courtesy Director of Antiquities Cyprus Museum)*

Paphos is the south-western corner of Cyprus and by nature is separated from the rest of the island by mountains. The main connection with the other towns is by the road to Limassol which runs in some places along the coast and goes inland from the rock of Aphrodite (Petra tou Romiou), climbing up a steep mountain, resembling a scene from a western film.

However, there have been times in the past when Paphos was more or less isolated from the rest of the island and developed its own identity, although communication was possible by land and sea. The fleets of the Greeks, Romans and, in later times, the Crusaders used Paphos as the natural harbour for rest and supplies: thus Paphos flourished through this trade and developed importance.

Although part of Paphos' history blends with the fortunes and misfortunes of the whole island, there are events which happened locally; these are worth mentioning, as they help the reader to understand Paphos, which is thought of as a living museum.

It is worthy of note that Paphos was important in the ancient Greek world and mentioned in the poems of Homer. This is mainly due to the fact that it was the centre for the worship of Aphrodite.

THE EARLY YEARS

Traces of human life in Paphos going back as far as the Neolithic and Chalcolithic periods around the middle of the 7th millenium BC, have been found in many places, the most important being at the villages of Lemba, Kissonerga, Yialia and Souskiou which are mainly of the 4th and 3rd millenium.

BRONZE (OR COPPER) AGE 2500 — 1500 BC

As in the rest of Cyprus, Paphos has seen tremendous changes at various times with settlers coming over from Greece, mainly Achaeans and Mycenean Greeks.

1500 — 1000 BC

Migration from the Greek cities continued and the kingdoms of Paphos (Paleapaphos) which eventually became the centre for the religion of Aphrodite (founded by Agapenor) and Marion were established, with other settlements at Maa-Paleokastron, Akamas, and around the harbour of Paphos.

During this period and mainly the 13th and 12th centuries, Paleapaphos was one of the island's major centres.

The Greek settlements remained well into the year 1000 BC and the settlers introduced a new way of life, which is still strongly in evidence today. The arrival of the Greek settlers was a time of great importance in the history of Paphos.

Left: Limestone female idol from Lemba. *Right:* Stealife idol: both from Chalcolithic period *(Courtesy Director of Antiquities Cyprus Museum).*

7

1000 — 700 BC

Phoenicians settled in parts of Cyprus.
As with the whole of the eastern Mediterranean Paphos suffered decline and many natural disasters. However, Paleapaphos retained its importance with the Kinyrad kings who ruled the kingdom and were also the High Priests of Aphrodite.
Cyprus was under the influence of Assyrian kings.

700 — 500 BC

Paphos re-emerged at this time as a commercial centre and economic relations were established, mainly with Assyria and Egypt. The Palaces of Nineveh of the Assyrian King Assharaddon were built with timber supplied by Eteandros, the King of Paphos. Short Egyptian rule of the island. In 545 the Cypriot kings submitted to the rule of Persia thus Cyprus became a centre of conflict between Greece & Persia as the Greeks considered Cyprus as part of the Greek world.

4TH AND 3RD CENTURIES BC

The wars between Greece and Persia entered a new phase with the emergence of Alexander the Great and his drive against the Persian might.
Paphos took positive action against the Persian rulers of Cyprus and supplied Alexander The Great with ships and men during the occupation and capture of Tyre. The mint of Paphos produced and supplied money to help the war effort.

According to archaeological evidence **Nea Paphos**, or Kato Paphos (the area in and around the harbour) was established as the commercial and administrative centre by King Nicocles c. 320BC. This coincided with the destruction of Marion (Polis) in 312BC, during the wars between the Antiochus of Asia Minor and Ptolemy of Egypt. The Ptolemy of Egypt was the victor and became the ruler of Cyprus. King Nicocles defended Paphos but eventually he was defeated. Legend says that he committed suicide with all the Family.

294—58BC — PTOLEMAIC RULE

The Ptolemaic rulers of Egypt, after their victory, took control of Paphos and the whole of Cyprus. The mint continued to expand and Nea Paphos became a very important centre, being accepted as the commercial and administrative centre of Cyprus. It also served as an important shipbuilding centre and as a naval base to the Ptolemaic navy.

Arts and commerce continued to flourish and Paphos became a very important cultural centre. The tale-writer Alexandros, the historian Istros and the poet Sopartos came to be some of the most famous men of the time.

An old engraving showing Paphos. In the far distance *(left)* is the harbour and castle.

58BC—330AD — THE ROMANS

The Romans conquered Cyprus. A pro-consul was appointed in Nea Paphos; the first administrator was called Cato.

During the Roman period Paphos remained the capital of Cyprus, both commercially and culturally. Cicero, the famous Roman orator, was a proconsul in Paphos from 51 to 50BC. The Greek language retained its importance as mosaics and coins show.

There was economic and political stability. Nea Paphos became the residence of the Roman proconsul, his administration, and the military headquarters. Surviving monuments including the famous mosaic floors of the administrative and residential house bear a testimony of the life of the city as an important centre.

During this period the religious centre remained at Paleapaphos *(see Chapter Two – the Mosaic Houses)*.

Paphos, which had reached the height of its importance under the Emperor Octavianus Augustus, was destroyed by a devasting earthquake around 15AD. The Emperor supervised the re-building of the town and also the Temple of Aphrodite at Palea-paphos. Paphos was also called the "Clau-dian Flavian Paphos" — the sacred metro-polis of Cities of Cyprus.

St. Paul visits Paphos

Paphos was involved in the new Christian religion in 45-46AD. The Apostles St. Paul, St. Mark and St. Barnabas reached Paphos during their visit to Cyprus. It was here that one of the most important incidents happened during the post-Christ period. Elymas, a prominent member of the Jewish community and advisor to the Governor, was alarmed by the interest being shown by the Roman Governor and tried to keep him away from St. Paul. St. Paul was punished by being tied to a column and given 39 lashes. In his anger St. Paul punished Elimas by blinding him. The Roman Governor was so impressed by St. Paul's teachings that he became the first Roman of high rank to become a Christian. The incident has no historical proof and is believed by some to be more fiction than

Roman Coin showing the sanctuary of Aphrodite *(Courtesy Cyprus Museum)*

9

fact, although it is true that St. Paul did succeed in converting the Roman Governor to Christianity. The Governor's name was Sergius Paulus. Many of the local people then followed the Governor's example and converted to Christianity. From this point Paphos became an important centre for Christian worship. As in all the other parts of the Roman Empire, Christianity became illegal and persecution by Roman Emperors followed over the next decades. Worship was carried out in secret in catacombs and other places such as Ayia Solomoni, Ayios Lambrianos and The Tombs of The Kings.

3RD AND 4TH CENTURIES

Strong earthquakes in 332 and 342 AD practically destroyed Nea Paphos, which fell into a decline. Salamis (in Famagusta) then became the capital of Cyprus. Cyprus became part of the new Byzantine Empire (or the Eastern Roman Empire as it was first called) and Christianity was the main religion.

However, the transfer of power from Paphos to Salamis was also due to a shift in strategy and other far-reaching changes by the first Christian Emperors.

This also resulted in Constantia (Salamis) taking the lead in ecclesiastical power despite the fact that Paphos had lead the island in the early years of Christian rule, as the largest Early Christian Basilica of Cyprus built in Paphos shows.

379-395

Severe penalities were imposed by the Byzantine Emperors on the worshippers of Aphrodite and those making sacrifices to idols.

648-963

Further suffering and destruction followed with successive Arab invasions, mainly by General Abdul Halign Kaif. Many monuments were almost totally destroyed and many treasures and slaves were taken away. Inhabitants fled from the port area and settled on the high ground, which is now the modern town of Ktima

965

The Arab raids were brought to an end by the Byzantine Emperor Nicephorus Phokas and peace followed.

11TH AND 12TH CENTURIES

Paphos saw normal life return to the area and there were periods of prosperity; this time was also the beginning of the Crusades. Many pilgrims landed in Paphos on their way to the Holy Land for rest and supplies. Some of them decided to stay and settle in Paphos, including the Duke of Savoy, Armendeus, and Erik I — the King of Denmark — who died here. By this time the Latins had become very powerful and influential.

1192-1489

This was the period when Cyprus was occupied by the Lusignans. Paphos was a very important commercial port and many wealthy Greeks and Franks stayed here. There emerged a struggle between the local Orthodox Christians and the Catholic Lusignans. The Latin Bishops established their seat in Paphos and the Greek Orthodox Bishop was exiled to the small town of Arsinoe (the new name of Marion, now Polis). The Lusignans established a Royal Domain and introduced their feudal system. All the land was given to the rich families and the peasants were forced to work in the fields. Sugar cane was one of the major products.

1372

Paphos became the centre of hostilities between the Lusignans and the Genoese, who were trying to occupy parts of Cyprus. A Cypriot chronicler called Leontius Machaeras describes:

"The Genoese called to their assistance many men of bad character. And there gathered together Bulgarians, Greeks and Tartars close upon 2000 men and they went and took the castle of Paphos . . . when the news of what the Genoese had done reached the capital (Nicosia), the king ordered that the Prince of Antioch should be made commander. He chose 1000 good fighting men and went to Paphos on Sunday the 3rd of July 1372. Early in the morning, the said Prince went to the tower of Paphos and began the attack. The enemy went into their galleys and came out from time to time and fought with him. The battle lasted for hours but to no avail because the Genoese had great help from the Bulgarians. The Prince's company did vast damage to the galleys but his expedition failed. The Prince went away and returned to Nicosia. And when the captains of the galleys learned that the Prince and his army had returned to Nicosia, they landed a company of men to collect slaves and they went and made captives in all the districts and took many men, women and children and they took away much food and cattle."

Paphos remained under Genoese rule until March of 1373 when hostilities ended and an armistice was declared between the Lusignans and Genoese in the whole of Cyprus.

1481

Felix Faber, a traveller, described Paphos: *"No longer a city but a miserable village built over ruins. The harbour being abandoned and ships only entering it when forced to do so, as was our fate . . ."*

1489-1571 AD — VENETIAN PERIOD

This was the period of Venetian occupation in Cyprus. Paphos became a more important port for supplying the Venetian fleet. A garrison was stationed near the harbour. It played an important role, as in previous years, in sugar production. But its decline started in the latter years of the Venetian Rule.

1571-1878

Cyprus entered a new era of occupation by the Ottoman Turks. Nicosia and Famagusta, which were nearer to Turkey, became more important places and Paphos was in continuing recession with the exception of certain agricultural areas which were allowed to keep going. Kato Paphos practically became a ghost town and Ktima (the modern city) emerged as the centre for administration. Dr. L. Ross said in 1845 — *Paphos port is a deserted, ugly, largely ruined place with a few inhabitants".*

As early as 1777, the census figures for that year show that Paphos had the smallest population in the island. As the Paphians were isolated from the rest of Cyprus they became much poorer than the other districts.

1821

Following the revolution in mainland Greece the Turkish administration in Cyprus carried out a purge which extended to Paphos and Bishop Chrysanthos, together with other prominent citizens, was executed.

1878

A new chapter opened in Cyprus' history. The British took over the occupation of the island from the Turks. Paphos, being situated far away from the administrative centres of Nicosia and Larnaca, remained a small town but grew in beauty with new administration buildings, a library, schools and green gardens and parks.

In the early years of the British rule and up to the late 50's the area was the slowest part of Cyprus to expand and it was well known as the place of "exile" for unpopular civil servants.

1960

After its struggle for independence Cyprus became a free nation and a member of the United Nations. Paphos gained fame once again since the first President of the Republic and world statesman, the late Archbishop Makarios, was born in the mountain village of Panayia. One of his aims was to bring Paphos closer to the rest of the island with new roads, small industries, expansion of agriculture and growth of the tourist industry. The expansion, which was halted briefly during the Turkish invasion of Cyprus in 1974, continued and the new refugees (since the August 1974 invasion) who came from the occupied north of Cyprus, together with the local people put all their energy and commercial expertise to work in new developments, new hotels and new industries.

With the establishment of new road networks, Paphos has become easily accessible from other parts of the island. The International airport has also contributed enormously in establishing Paphos as an important tourist centre in the eastern Mediterranean.

28th October Square with the Library and Police Station *(Right)*.

PAPHOS TOWN

Modern Paphos — Kennedy Square and entrance to Makarios Avenue.

Today Paphos includes two main towns. The modern town of **KTIMA,** built on a rocky plateau overlooking the sea, which is the capital of the district; and **KATO PAPHOS** (Lower Paphos) which is the ancient city around the harbour (this area was known as Nea Paphos), plus the new town built to the east of the harbour with hotels, apartment blocks, restaurants, etc. Please note that the whole area is now merged into one, run by the same munincipality. However, to make it easier for the visitor to explore the place, we describe each one separately.

KTIMA (PANO PAPHOS = Upper Paphos)

This town was first established by the fleeing inhabitants of Nea Paphos during the first Arab raids and at that time it became an agricultural centre with large farms. However, there is evidence that people were living here prior to this, as discovered tombs have shown. The word Ktima means property. During the Frankish period of the Lusignans many people came here to settle among the beautiful orchids. The town's main function and the reason for its importance that it is the commercial, cultural and administrative centre for the Paphos district. In the narrow streets of the shopping centre one can buy practically everything and, although most of the shops do not have vast window displays, one should not hesitate to go inside and inquire about a particular item, although in most cases prices are displayed.

The fruit and vegetable market is to be found at the end of Makarios III Avenue. The market is covered and the nearby street is paved and has retained its old character.

The town itself does not possess important archaeological sites, but there are, nevertheless, some very interesting places. Over the years tombs of various periods have been discovered during building work with burial artefacts.

13

MAIN PLACES OF INTEREST

(1) HELLINOSPHILLIOS
This locality situated near the old Chiftlik of Basilikon at the north east of the town near the road to Konia and near the New Hospital is unknown even to many locals. Interesting rock-hewn tombs of Hellenistic-Roman years were found here; of a unique type in Cyprus, similar to others found in North Africa, Palestine and Syria. It is believed they were later used by early Christians as tombs and chapels.

Excavations took place many years ago of some tombs but the place was abandoned and sadly, has not been well looked after.

(2) AYIOS PAVLOS CHURCH
A new church, dominating the northern part of the town, to the left of the main road to Polis. A modern church built in 1970, based on the traditional Byzantine style.

(3) AYIOS KENDEAS CHURCH
Situated behind the Public buildings, the church was built around 1930. The exterior is not of great importance but the interior contains some older wood carvings including a wooden iconostacy, the bishop's throne and a few 19th century icons.

(4) AYIOS THEODOROS CATHEDRAL
This is the oldest surviving church of Ktima, built in 1896 and is next to the Metropolis. A new archway extension was built in 1988 and the square outside was paved and closed to the traffic.

A memorial column stands in one corner commemorating the victims of the Turkish purge in 1821. They included the Paphian Bishop Chrysanthos and others.

The interior of the church is simple except that the iconostasi contains some old icons.

(5) THE BISHOP'S PALACE (Metropolis)
This beautifully designed building is the seat of the Bishop of Paphos and is next to the church of Ayios Theodoros.

It was built in 1910 by the Bishop of Paphos Iakovos and underwent extensions and improvements in later years. The present Bishop Chrysostomos expanded the buildings with new offices and exhibition halls.

Here is the collection of the Metropolis. The various religious objects include rare books such as a Bible dated to 1472, and

An old photo taken at Kennedy Square. A lot has changed since then. *(Photo unknown).*

14

others of the 16th, 17th and 18th centuries. Important is the collection of Codes and Rules of the Turkish Rulers. There are numerous rare manuscripts.

(6) THE BYZANTINE MUSEUM OF THE HOLY SEE OF PAPHOS

1 Illysion St. Tel. 232092/232361 and Exo Vrysis

Of great importance is the icon collection, one of the best in the island, many of them collected from isolated churches of the Paphos district and restored. They include "The Virgin Eleousa", "Virgin Philochiotissa", "St. Nicholas", "the execution of St. John the Baptist" and many others some going back to the 14th century.

(7) PRIVATE ETHNOGRAPHICAL MUSEUM OF PROFESSOR G.S. ELIADES

This museum is situated at No. 1 Exo Vrysis Street, between Palamas Square and the Bishopric Palace. There is a fine collection of bygones of Cyprus, from the Neolithic period to today. They are delightfully displayed in a charming house full of character both inside and out. A rock cut tomb is open to the public, situated at the far end of an open courtyard. Rooms show the way peasants used to live, their clothes, etc. and there is a bedroom, kitchen and working room. They include folk art,

Right: An impressive woodcarving and paintings of a "door" from the church of Timios Stavros — Arminou *(Paphos Byzantine Museum).*
Below: The southern wing of the Bishop's Palace.

15

carved chests, baskets, pottery; also a number of ancient coins and other artefacts. The museum is open daily and again, well worth visiting.

Entrance fee and conducted tours, Tel. 232010.

Above: The courtyard and entrance to the Byzantine Museum from the Exo Vrysis area.
Below: An icon of a saint from the Byzantine Museum. *(Courtesy Byzantine Museum).*

One of the many exhibition rooms of George Eliades museum.

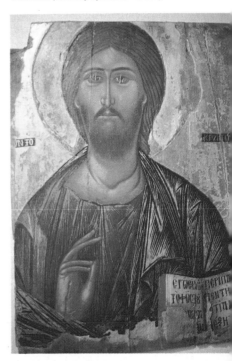

(8) THE PAPHOS DISTRICT MUSEUM

The Museum is situated at the far end of Leoforos George Grivas Dhigheni towards Yeroskipos. It is a small museum housed in a modern building but it has a very fine collection covering the entire Paphos district from as far back as the Neolithic period, through the Bronze Age, Hellenistic, Roman and Byzantine times. The museum is open daily but check for opening hours.

There are at present 5 rooms with plans for further extensions. The collection is arranged chronologically.

The 1st room is dedicated to the Chalcolithic, Neolithic and Bronze Age periods.

The 2nd to the Iron Age and the Classical period and shows statues, tombstones, inscriptions etc.

In the 3rd room there are objects from the Hellenistic and Roman period. These contain statues *(including two large Venuses)*, lamps, terracotta figurines, also clay hot water bottles etc.

The 4th room exhibits items from the late Roman and early Christian periods.

The newly added 5th room contains items of the Byzantine and Medieval Frankish periods which includes clay pots, tombstones and an interesting Renaissance statue.

In all, this small museum provides a unique collection of Paphos history. Stones, statues and other material is also housed under cover on the eastern side of the gardens.

— George Grivas Dhigenis Avenue Tel. 230215/240215.

Opening Hours:

Summer:	Daily	7.30—13.30
	Sunday	10.00—13.00
Winter:	Daily	8.00—14.00
		15.30—17.30
	Sunday	10.00—13.00

Various exhibits of statues including the two well known Aphrodite's from the Museum's Collection.

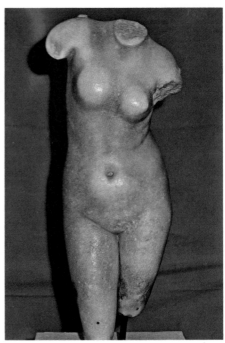

Above left: Medieval statues from the Frankish Cathedral.
Above right: Aphrodite's statue of Greco-Roman period. *Below:* Exhibits of vases, pots and other items.

THE SQUARES AND OTHER PLACES

Front view of Nicolaïdion School.

(9) 28th OCTOBER SQUARE

This is the most impressive square of the town, as all traffic goes through it, (it cannot be avoided). The dominating feature is a single high column of Corinthian style erected as a monument to the Greek Heroes who fought in the Albanian War when Italy invaded Greece on the 28th October 1940. It also commemorates the Paphian dead who volunteered to go and fight with the Greek forces.

The Square, and some of the surrounding buildings as well as the narrow, long park with its columns and fountains was built by one of Paphos' most energetic and popular Mayors who served from 1943-1953 — Galatopoulos.

The Buildings around the square include:

(10) THE LIBRARY

This small public Library on the west side of the square was built in 1946 and contains books in Greek. A special room has books in English and French mainly of literature, history and poetry.

Some modern books have been added to the Library which is used by many students and citizens as well as the small community of British residents who have settled in Paphos.

It is open daily in the mornings and some afternoons. Tel. 232010.

(11) THE POLICE STATION

Situated to the north western side and built in British Colonial style, it was the centre of the British rule of Paphos. Now it is the Central Police Station of Paphos district.

THE SCHOOLS & STADIUM situated to the north and north east of the square include from west to east:—

(12) DEMETRIOS ELEMENTARY SCHOOL

This was built in 1928 by a Paphian who emigrated to America and is used by children 6-12 years. The facade is of Neo Classical style. In later years other buildings were added at the back.

(13) IAKOVION STADIUM & SPORTS CENTRE

The entrance gates of the stadium were built in the Neoclassical style by the energetic Bishop of Paphos Iacovos Antzoulatos, in the 1920's. The stadium is used by students, individuals and the

19

Paphos athletic club (the oldest in Cyprus) KORIVOS. Various events take place in there, from sports, athletics, football and other events.

(14) NICOLAIDION SCHOOL (Gymnasium)

A higher education school building is to the east of the stadium entrance and was built by Nicolas I. Nicolaides who was Mayor of Paphos 1920-1943. His bust is in the foreground together with Paschalis Paschalides, the first headmaster of the school and Loizos Philippou, one of Paphos' best known benefactors. He first published the "Paphos" newspaper at the turn of the century and he donated his library to the school which is now housed here. Amongst the many books there are some books and many interesting magazines and papers relating to Paphos district.

(15) THE FIRST GYMNASIUM (Makarios Gymnasium)

Originally this was an extension of the Nicolaidion School to house the increasing numbers of secondary students and it was completed in 1960. During the construction many ancient burial tombs were discovered here.

A bas-relief, built to commemorate the students contribution to the struggle of independence 1955-59, shows a student fighting a lion representing the British Colonial Administration.

The main feature of the building is a central hall which is used for lectures, recitals and plays.

(16) THE TOWN HALL

This is to the east of the square and it was completed in 1955. It houses the Mayor and the munincipality of Paphos. Exhibitions of Paintings and other events take place in the large hall.

(17) THE PUBLIC GARDENS

On the eastern side of the square, these small gardens are nicely laid out and also contain a tennis court and a children's playground. An ideal place to rest.

(18) COSTIS PALAMAS SQUARE

To the south of 28th October Square, is a much smaller square which has two interesting features. To the north east, is the southern entrance to the Gardens, dominated by square column gates and inside is the bust of **COSTIS PALAMAS** one of Greece's most famous modern poets. It was established in 1951.

The other is the **EROS POOL**, a circular pool surrounded by columns and covered with a dome. In the centre is a replica of the

Costis Palamas Square and southern entrance to the Park. The bust of the poet was the work of sculptor Tombros.

20

The entrance "gate" — to Iakovion Stadium and Sports Centre.

Sleeping Eros statue (original in the Cyprus Museum — Nicosia). Trees add to the aesthetic appeal of the square.

(19) MOUSALLAS SQUARE (Akropolis)
To the south of Costis Palamas, after the Bishopric, this square is dominated by a central structure — a restaurant and is important for its magnificent panoramic views of the town and countryside below stretching to the coastline.

The hill is strewn with loose rocks and is dangerous to climb down.

(20) EXO VRISI
On the eastern side of Mousallas a path takes you to the most picturesque place of old Christian Ktima. It can also be reached from the Ethnographical Museum.

A narrow street leads into other narrow streets and small houses built on the side of the hill with beautiful gardens. These form a miniature *Plaka* (of Athens).

It houses a couple of residential artists and is an interesting place to explore especially in the spring.

The main feature which unfortunately has become rather indistinguished is the small **fountain** which still has running water at all times of the year. In the old days it was the meeting place for people and the animals and a focal point of the area.

(21) KENNEDY SQUARE
A small square to the west of 28th October Square, named after the late American President, has roads leading in all directions. It has no important features except that it is surrounded by kafenia, where you can relax with a drink; best known is *'Peggy's Cafe'*. It is run by a well known Irish lady who came here, loved Paphos and took over the place thus giving an excellent service to the many tourists, locals and British ex-patriates.

All the main taxi offices are also around or near the square.

To the west is the entrance to the main shopping road, Makarios Avenue, which leads to the munincipal market.

(22) 9th MARCH SQUARE
To the south east of the market, this square is dominated on the eastern side by the Public Buildings. Built in Colonial style, they include the District Land Office, the District Courts, the District Administration Offices and the Central Post Office.

On the north western side and below the hill are the remains of the old Turkish **BATHS** (Hamam). After they ceased to

The Cupid Temple at Palamas Square. Inside rests a copy of the statuette of sleeping Eros.

function as Baths they were used to House the Museum until it was moved to the present site. Unfortunately this interesting building has been neglected and is covered with trees.

(23) THE DISTRICT OFFICER'S RESIDENCE

On the eastern side of the town, next to the Museum is the residence of the District Officer of Paphos.

Built originally by the British for the District administrator who had absolute power in the day to day life of the district. It is a large house built in the true colonial style with extensive gardens and a tennis court.

Above: The Baths undergoing a restoration programme. *Below:* The picturesque Exo Vrisi area.

(24) MOUTTALLOS

This was the old medieval area of Ktima which was a Domain Royale and it was inhabited by the wealthy Latins and Greeks who had a good lifestyle.

After the Turkish occupation the town around the harbour was abandoned and the Turkish administration took over this part of the town of Ktima which is called *Mouttallos*. Turkish settlers also arrived. The Christian church of Ayia Sophia became a mosque and still survives today. The Christians and Greek inhabitants eventually moved eastwards (where the main town now is) and the Turks remained here until 1974-75 when they went to the Northern part of the island.

Now the place houses Greek Cypriot refugees from the north but it still retains its narrow streets and low old houses. Unknown to most tourists it provides a few traditional tavernas where local dishes, not always available in the more modern areas, are available and at reasonable prices.

(25) THE MARKET

This is for meat and fish, but its fresh fruit and vegetables bring colour to the area. Mainly on Saturdays, the market expands into the surrounding streets where villagers bring in their own produce which they display on the road. Here many bargains can be made. The site is very colourful with

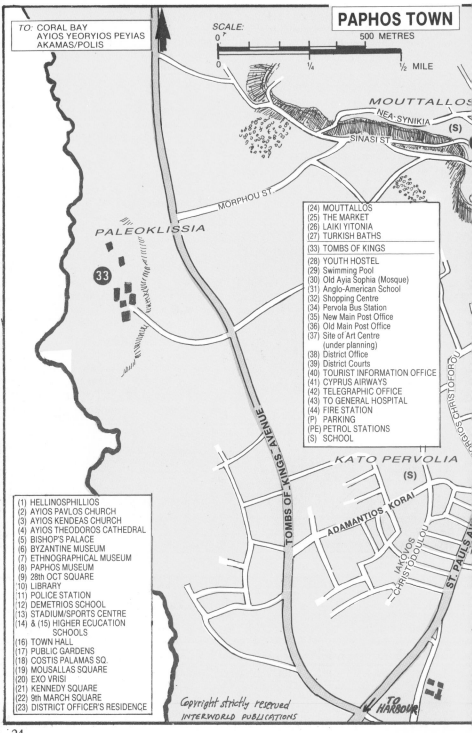

PAPHOS TOWN

TO: CORAL BAY
AYIOS YEORYIOS PEYIAS
AKAMAS/POLIS

SCALE:

500 METRES

½ MILE

MOUTTALLOS

NEA·SYNIKIA

(S)

SINASI ST.

MORPHOU ST.

PALEOKLISSIA

33

TOMBS OF KINGS AVENUE

KATO PERVOLIA

(S)

ADAMANTIOS KORAI

IAKOVOS CHRISTODOULOU

GEORGIOS CHRISTOFOROU

ST. PAUL'S AVE

TO HARBOUR

(24) MOUTTALLOS
(25) THE MARKET
(26) LAIKI YITONIA
(27) TURKISH BATHS

(33) TOMBS OF KINGS

(28) YOUTH HOSTEL
(29) Swimming Pool
(30) Old Ayia Sophia (Mosque)
(31) Anglo-American School
(32) Shopping Centre
(34) Pervola Bus Station
(35) New Main Post Office
(36) Old Main Post Office
(37) Site of Art Centre
      (under planning)
(38) District Office
(39) District Courts
(40) TOURIST INFORMATION OFFICE
(41) CYPRUS AIRWAYS
(42) TELEGRAPHIC OFFICE
(43) TO GENERAL HOSPITAL
(44) FIRE STATION
(P) PARKING
(PE) PETROL STATIONS
(S) SCHOOL

(1) HELLINOSPHILLIOS
(2) AYIOS PAVLOS CHURCH
(3) AYIOS KENDEAS CHURCH
(4) AYIOS THEODOROS CATHEDRAL
(5) BISHOP'S PALACE
(6) BYZANTINE MUSEUM
(7) ETHNOGRAPHICAL MUSEUM
(8) PAPHOS MUSEUM
(9) 28th OCT SQUARE
(10) LIBRARY
(11) POLICE STATION
(12) DEMETRIOS SCHOOL
(13) STADIUM/SPORTS CENTRE
(14) & (15) HIGHER ECUCATION
          SCHOOLS
(16) TOWN HALL
(17) PUBLIC GARDENS
(18) COSTIS PALAMAS SQ.
(19) MOUSALLAS SQUARE
(20) EXO VRISI
(21) KENNEDY SQUARE
(22) 9th MARCH SQUARE
(23) DISTRICT OFFICER'S RESIDENCE

TO: CHLORAKA VILLAGE
CORAL BAY
EMBA
AYIOS NEOPHYTOS MON

TO THE NORTH:
AYIOS NEOPHYTOS MON.
KHRYSORROYIATISSA MON.
POLIS/BATHS OF APHRODITE
MOUNTAINS

TO: KONIA/MARATHOUNTA
EPISKOPI

TO THE EAST:
YEROSKIPOS VILLAGE
PAPHOS AIRPORT
TEMPLE OF APHRODITE
LIMASSOL

25

lots of fresh fruit and vegetables. It is advisable to visit the market early in the morning.

(26) LAIKI YITONIA

The old shops around the market have been restored and some of the streets paved. Various items are displayed including lace, artifacts, souvenirs etc. Colourful and popular is Mr George's shop but retirement may deprive the tourists of his warmth.

Various cafes around the area provide late morning refreshments and lunch, Souvlaki in pitta (kebabs) and traditional Cypriot cooking.

Above: A view of Laiki Yitonia. *Below:* The outside area of the vegetable market.
Left: A view of Mouttallos area of old Paphos — viewed from the market.

26

Shopping in the old town of Paphos is very enjoyable. *Above:* Mr. George, a typical shopkeeper and a real character, the star attraction of the area. *Below:* A souvenir shop along the main Makarios Avenue shopping street. Jewellery, clothes and shoe shops are plentiful.

KATO PAPHOS ANCIENT NEA PAPHOS

The picturesque harbour of Kato Paphos.

Nea Paphos, well-known to the natives as KATO PAPHOS, is situated about two miles south of Paphos town (Ktima). It was established as a major town with fortifications and was also an important port during the 4th Century BC. This was due to the fact that King Nicocles of Palea Paphos moved the political and commercial activities to the new town. However, the port was active before the 4th Century BC, since the pilgrims to the Holy Temple of Aphrodite, seven miles to the east at Paleapaphos, disembarked here. It is believed that the town was founded in 1180 BC by Agapenor. The port and surrounding area flourished during the Hellenistic, Ptolemaic and Roman periods. The whole area is scattered with remains of the past, an archaeological paradise for any visitor.

It is also worth mentioning here that it is believed that the ancient harbour during the Hellenistic and Roman times covered the area from the existing harbour to the area of Moulia rocks to the South East. British underwater Army divers surveyed the area in 1959 and discovered traces of the old harbour and breakwater walls, now submerged under deep water. The inside harbour extended up the hill to the Byzantine Castle and up to the area where the Basilica Gardens Apartments are situated.

Many of the places described in the following pages are within walking distance from most hotels and apartments and some are connected with a bus service. Alternatively, a taxi will take you to the place or places of your choice and collect you afterwards. Excavations continue all the time.

The last Cinyraid King of Paleapaphos moved his headquarters here in c. 320BC and established a new town and a larger harbour which later served the Ptolemies, the Romans, the Crusaders and the Latins. During the Ptolemaic and Roman periods it was the capital of Cyprus and it saw great prosperity and served both fleets.

During the Byzantine period it suffered from extensive Arab raids and after the raids of Abu-l-Awar in 653, monuments and churches were destroyed. A garrison of about 12,000 men stayed here up to the 680's.

It was revived during the medieval Lusignan conquest of Cyprus between 12-16th centuries and the harbour played an important role in the communications and the supplies of ships for the Crusaders and the Genoese fleet. Thus a commercial and military presence was established and buildings, churches and the Latin Cathedral were amongst the best in Cyprus; sadly however nothing remains. Systematic excavations started in 1951 and continued ever since have unearthed very interesting ruins, however many more are still covered and the area is protected from buildings.

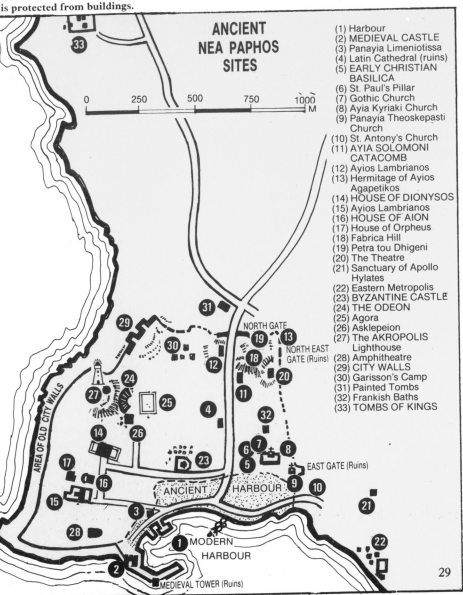

ANCIENT NEA PAPHOS SITES

0   250   500   750   1000 M

(1) Harbour
(2) MEDIEVAL CASTLE
(3) Panayia Limeniotissa
(4) Latin Cathedral (ruins)
(5) EARLY CHRISTIAN BASILICA
(6) St. Paul's Pillar
(7) Gothic Church
(8) Ayia Kyriaki Church
(9) Panayia Theoskepasti Church
(10) St. Antony's Church
(11) AYIA SOLOMONI CATACOMB
(12) Ayios Lambrianos
(13) Hermitage of Ayios Agapetikos
(14) HOUSE OF DIONYSOS
(15) Ayios Lambrianos
(16) HOUSE OF AION
(17) House of Orpheus
(18) Fabrica Hill
(19) Petra tou Dhigeni
(20) The Theatre
(21) Sanctuary of Apollo Hylates
(22) Eastern Metropolis
(23) BYZANTINE CASTLE
(24) THE ODEON
(25) Agora
(26) Asklepeion
(27) The AKROPOLIS Lighthouse
(28) Amphitheatre
(29) CITY WALLS
(30) Garisson's Camp
(31) Painted Tombs
(32) Frankish Baths
(33) TOMBS OF KINGS

NORTH GATE
NORTH EAST GATE (Ruins)
EAST GATE (Ruins)
AREA OF OLD CITY WALLS
ANCIENT HARBOUR
MODERN HARBOUR
MEDIEVAL TOWER (Ruins)

29

PLACES OF INTEREST

(1) THE HARBOUR

Up to the 1960's some small cargo boats used to anchor just off the harbour and barges transported local produce to the boats. This consisted of carobs, almonds, sultanas etc. Timber, cement and other materials and goods were brought to shore. No such boats call here any more. Limassol harbour is used instead.

However, the harbour is full of colourful fishing boats and at times many yachts from all over Europe anchor at the jetty. This was completed in 1959 and officially opened by the last British Governor of Cyprus Sir Hugh Foot.

It is an ideal area for the visitor to enjoy a stroll along the promenade or relax in the numerous tavernas with a refreshing drink or a fish meal.

In ancient times, especially during the Ptolemaic and Roman periods it was full of commercial activity but in later years it has declined and even been completely abandoned several times.

(2) THE MEDIEVAL CASTLE

Commanding a view of the southern part of

Above: The Pelican, the permanent visitor of Paphos harbour. *Below:* Paphos Harbour.

30

the harbour is the Medieval Castle, which is visible from all directions. It was built by the Lusignans in the 13th Century AD to replace the destroyed Byzantine Castle. It was partially destroyd by the defending Venetians in 1570 AD, but the Turkish victors restored and fortified it soon afterwards.

The extension, which is further along the breakwater, is in ruins since it was never restored. Above the entrance to the Castle is an Arabic saying written in 1592 — "By the Goodness of God, the Honourable Ahmet Pasha — Hafouz of the Truthful Koran — erected the Castle of Paphos and left a Good Religious Work. This very strong castle. May God Benefit his establisher said . . ." (Atel is the name of the poet who wrote the inscription.) KALAI BAFTIR BIR HISNI HASIN — translated it means — *The Castle of Paphos is a very Strong Castle.* The Castle is now restored and open to the public. You can explore the various rooms and chambers which were used as prisons and housed the garrison. Under the British it was used as salt stores. From the top one can enjoy a

wonderful view of the harbour and surrounding area.

Extending eastwards and now in ruins were further fortifications and a smaller castle.

Right and *Below:* Two views of the castle which dominates the harbour.

(3) PANAYIA LIMENIOTISSA

The remains of this early Christian Basilica lie very close to the harbour and just behind the restaurants. The original church dates back to the 5th century AD and is dedicated to Panayia Limeniotissa (Our Lady of The Port). Floor mosaics and wall foundations can be seen from the road.

(4) THE LATIN CATHEDRAL (GALATARIOTISSA)

Another impressive church, which was unfortunately destroyed. It was built in the Gothic style around the 14th Century and later restored by Francesco Contarini, the Last Latin Bishop of Paphos, who was removed after the Turkish occupation. Nothing now remains of this Cathedral, except one thick column.

The name GALATARIOTISSA means the Virgin Mary of Milk. Thus the church is dedicated to pregnant women so that they ensure supply of their milk for their babies.

(5) EARLY CHRISTIAN BASILICA CHURCH

The church which now stands on this site and is of architectural interest is called AYIA KYRIAKI, built around the 13th Century in typical Byzantine style: it is open to the public. The church was built on the remains of an earlier Basilica built in the 4th Century AD was one of the largest in Cyprus and with seven aisles reduced later to five, including floors and huge granite columns which can be seen at the side of the existing church.

The narthex and atrium were on the western side and having porticoes and open court around it.

Some of the floors show paving in interesting geometric mosaics. Further excavations continue and the area is not open to the public; however, the remains can be seen clearly from the road.

(6) ST. PAULS PILLAR

The pillar, which is believed to be that of St. Paul, can be seen to the west of Ayia Kyriaki Church. This pillar has a special significance since it was alleged that during his visit to Paphos in 45 AD to preach Christianity, St. Paul was bound to it as

The remains of the Latin Cathedral.

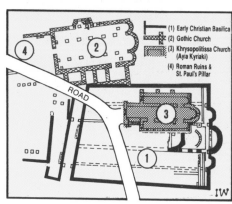

(1) Early Christian Basilica
(2) Gothic Church
(3) Khrysopolitissa Church (Ayia Kyriaki)
(4) Roman Ruins & St. Paul's Pillar

Plan of the Early Christian Basilica and Gothic Cathedral.

punishment and given 39 lashes — "Saranta para mia" — as the Greeks say to this day. Afterwards, in his anger, St. Paul punished the local Jewish religious leader, Elymas —who masterminded the punishment — by blinding him.

The Roman Governor, Sergius-Paulus, was then converted to Christianity, thus becoming the first important Roman in the whole Empire to embrace the new religion. The surrounding remains are thought to be those of the Roman Forum.

(7) GOTHIC CHURCH

The remains of the Gothic Church are to the south east of St Paul's Pillar and close to the Christian Basilica on the other side of the road. This church, built in Latin style around 1300 AD, was probably used by the Franciscan Convent of Paphos. Some Renaissance-style statues found here date back to the 15th Century. When the Turks occupied Cyprus the church was turned into a Mosque but it collapsed towards the end of the 16th Century. The floor remains and some walls can be seen.

(8) AYIA KYRIAKI CHURCH

Also mentioned above (No. 5) stands in-between the Gothic Church and the old Basilica. In fact it was built over its ruins. When the Turks took over Cyprus it changed from a Latin to an Orthodox church.

Various additions were made over the years including the Bell Tower built at the turn of the century. The church interior is simple but contains an interesting iconostasi.

(9) PANAYIA THEOSKEPASTI

Very close to Ayia Kyriaki stands the impressive church of Panayia Theoskepasti (All Holy Virgin Mary), protected by God. It is built on a rock, probably the part of the eastern city walls and during the Arab raids it is said that a miraculous cloud covered

A painting showing **St. Paul** *(left)* blinding **Elymas** *(right)* while the Roman governor **Sergius Paulus** *(centre)* watches with astonishment; he then converted to Christianity.
This most important early Christian event gave strength and expansion to Christianity in Paphos and Cyprus.

Below: The remains of the Early Christian Basilica next to Ayia Kyriaki Church.

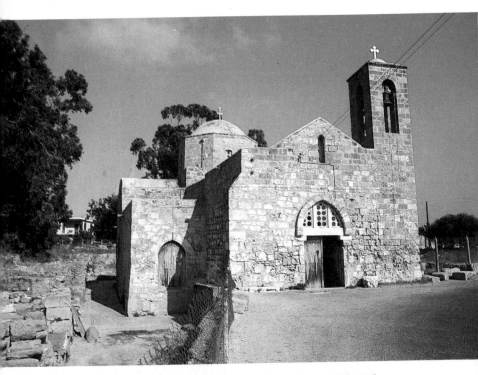

Above: Ayia Kyriaki Church; *Below:* The church of Panayia Theoskepasti.

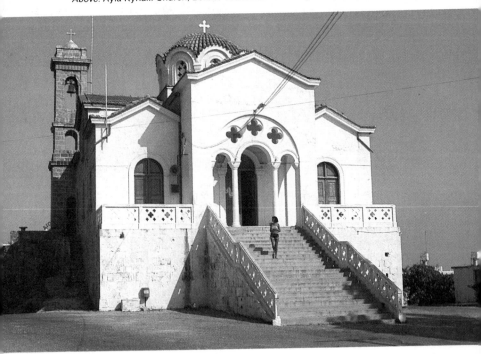

the church, thus rendering it invisible to the enemy.

When one Saracen invader came into the Church and tried to take gold and other offerings around the icon of the Virgin, a miracle occurred to protect them. A sword appeared and cut off the Saracen's hands. This scene can be seen painted on one icon. It is also believed to be the church of the "Shrouded Madonna". The existing church was built in 1922, after the original one was destroyed.

The church is open to the public and visitors to it will enjoy the beautiful icons and interior decorations.

(10) ST. ANTHONY'S CHURCH

This small church is in St. Anthony Street and is leased out by the Bishopric of Paphos to the Anglican Church for regular services by the British community of Paphos.

(11) AYIA SOLOMONI CATACOMB

This well known catacomb, unique of its type in Cyprus, lies along the main road to Kato Paphos, south of Fabrica Hill and close to the Apollo Hotel. Steps lead down from an open courtyard to underground caves carved deep into the earth.

The origin of the catacomb goes back to the Hellenistic period and was also used at later dates. Originally, it is believed it was used

Above: The church of Panayia Theoskepasti as seen from the rear, built on rock, which was part of the Eastern city fortifications.

Below: St. Antony's church. Photo taken before buildings surrounded the church.

as a burial ground but in later times as a refuge for people, mainly Christians, during the Roman persecutions. It was at that time that it was dedicated to Ayia Solomoni and it became a church and place of worship. The legend explains that Solomoni, a devoted Christian mother was pursued by the Romans, found refuge with her sons in a catacomb. The Romans when they discovered her hiding place, sealed off the caves and she was buried there with her sons.

There is another version though which says that Solomoni (Hannah) was Jewish and living in Palestine. Her seven children were tortured to death in Palestine by the Romans, around 168 AD. The local Jews established this as her synagogue which was later abandoned and used by the Christians for protection. As a chapel and place of worship the chambers were decorated with impressive wall paintings during the 12th Century AD, but most of these have been damaged by the weather. Names of Crusader soldiers were scratched on both the paintings and the walls, thus inflicting more damage. Further steps lead down to a Holy Well. The catacomb is open to both worshippers and the general public.

(12) AYIOS LAMBRIANOS

This catacomb lies on the other side of the road from Ayia Solomoni, and opposite the Apollo Hotel. There is an open courtyard, surrounded by chambers and graves, similar to other tombs in the area.

(13) THE HERMITAGE OF AYIOS AGAPETIKOS

This interesting cave, hewn out of rock above ground, lies on the eastern slopes of Fabrica Hill and is one of the earliest Christian monuments in Paphos. Apart from being a religious area it is also dedicated to the Protector of Lovers (Ayios Agapetikos). Even today lovers go to the cave to light a candle and pray.

Above Top: The entrance to the catacomb of Ayia Solomini.
Centre: Ayios Agapetikos Hermitage.
Right: Ayios Lambrianos.

These are probably the most interesting places to visit in Paphos. They exhibit some of the most fascinating floor mosaics, not only to be found in Cyprus but the whole of the Mediterranean.

Currently they consist of different locations; the Houses are all situated close to each other and given names according to the main themes of their mosaic scenes and are situated between the harbour and the Lighthouse.

It will not surprise anybody if more mosaic floors are still to be uncovered under the debris of the ruined houses.

It is interesting to point out that although the mosaics are of the Roman period, they are inscribed with Greek writing.

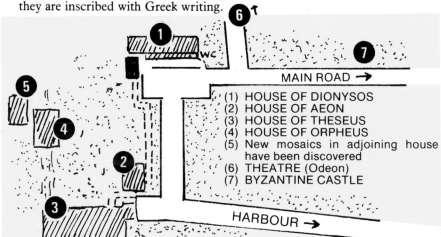

MAIN ROAD →

(1) HOUSE OF DIONYSOS
(2) HOUSE OF AEON
(3) HOUSE OF THESEUS
(4) HOUSE OF ORPHEUS
(5) New mosaics in adjoining house have been discovered
(6) THEATRE (Odeon)
(7) BYZANTINE CASTLE

HARBOUR →

(14) THE HOUSE OF DIONYSOS

It is believed that this was once a private house (roman villa) and dates back to the second half of the 2nd Century AD. It was accidentally discovered in 1962 by a farmer ploughing his fields. This house is of enormous importance since most of the floors have mosaic scenes depicting characters from Greek mythology, and their artistic value places them amongst the finest in the world. This house is so beautiful that it is visited by art lovers from all over the world. The United States Aid Mission helped with finance to erect the protective shelter.

Some of the mosaic scenes include the following:

The Triumph of Dionysos

Dionysos, God of Wine and Happiness, sits crowned with vine leaves in a chariot drawn by two wild beasts. Following behind is a satyr with an amphora full of wine, Pan, a young negro and two maenads. More figures can be seen in front of the chariot and the last figure is that of a young man sounding a trumpet:— "The Triumph of Dionysos".

It occupies the centre of the mosaic area and it is the longest.

Dionysos, Akme and Ikarios

Here the God is seated on a stool offering grapes to Nymph Akme, who is drinking from a bowl (wine, of course!). Next to her Ikarios is leading an ox-driven cart loaded with flasks full of wine. Behind the cart are two drunken men — *"The First Wine Drinkers"* - as the inscription above them explains. According to legend Dionysos visited the Palace of the King of Athens, Ikarios, where he taught him the art of making wine.

While the King was taking the wine to the Athenians he met with two shepherds, to whom he offered a drink, They were not

Above: THE TRIUMPH OF DIONYSOS.
Below: DIONYSOS — AKME — IKARIOS and the first Wine Drinkers — one of the most impressive mosaics.
(Courtesy Director of Antiquities)

used to wine and, once they became drunk they thought the King was trying to poison them and they killed him.

Pyramus and Thisbe

This mosaic shows Thisbe standing frightened staring at a panther (wild beast) that is running away, carrying a cloth in its mouth. Pyramus, crowned with reeds, lies dying on the ground holding a cornucopia. Here the legend says that Pyramus and Thisbe were two lovers who were forbidden by their parents to marry. One day Thisbe, on her way to their meeting place, was attacked by a wild beast. She was injured but managed to escape. Unfortunately she left behind a blood-stained veil. When Pyramus arrived at the scene he found the

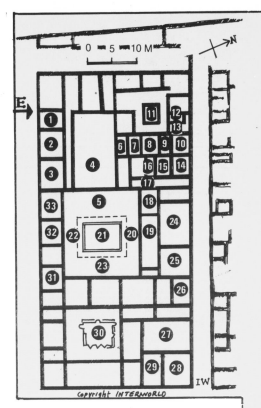

HOUSE OF DIONYSOS

E = ENTRANCE TO MOSAICS

(1) SCYLLA MOSAIC — A mythical sea monster (part woman, part fish, part dog).
— *The only mosaic not in its original position, being transferred from another building.*

(2) NARCISSUS — Looking at his reflection in a pool of water.

(3) THE FOUR SEASONS —

(4) THE TABLINUM — the largest room and most important.

(5) PYRAMOS & THISBE
(First Panel Room)
ICAROS & DIONYSOS
NEPTUNE & ANEMONY
APOLLO & DAPHNE
(Western Portico)

(6) — (16) LIVING QUARTERS
Workshops, Kitchens etc.

(17) GEOMETRIC SCENES
in black & white

(18) PHAEDRA & HIPPOLYTOS

(19) LONG HALL — Polychrome geometric patterns and other motifs.

(20) NORTHERN PORTICO
Hunting scenes.

(21) ATRIUM — a central open court — colonnaded portico opened on all four sides providing light.

(22) EASTERN PORTICO
Hunting scenes.

(23) SOUTHERN PORTICO
Hunting scenes.

(24) LONG ROOM — Polychrome geometric patterns.

(25) THE RAPE OF GANYMEDES

(26) BATHS & IATRINES

(27) (28) (29) PRIVATE ROOMS
perhaps bedrooms — floors covered with small pebbles set in mortar.

(30) OPEN ATRIUM — was surrounded with a collonate.

(31) MOSAICS with black & white geometric patterns.

(32) MOSAICS with multiple geometric panels.

(33) ROOM OF THE PEACOCK.

---

veil and, believing that his love had been killed, he took his own life. Later Thisbe returned and found Pyramus lying dead. In her grief she also killed herself.

This dramatic Love Story was recreated by Shakespeare in his plays *"Midsummer Night's Dream"* and *"Romeo and Juliet"*. A love tragedy, also used by other writers.

Daphne-Peneus-Apollo
Here is a scene of Daphne with her voluptuous, naked body standing and holding a veil over her head. To the right is APOLLO, God of Music and Hunting who loved Daphne and when he started chasing her, she asked Zeus for help and rescued her from amorous Apollo.

Zeus, responding to her wish, transformed her into a Laurel. The scene shows her in the process of rooting into earth and changing into the laurel *(daphne);* then Apollo's favourite tree. On the spot lies her father Peneus, God of Rivers.

Silver Ptolemaic coins as found at the House of Dionysos. *(Courtesy Director of Antiquities).*

Above: THISBE and PYRAMUS — a scene of the love tragedy, an outstanding mosaic scene. *(Courtesy of Director of Antiquities).*

Above: PHAEDRA and HIPPOLYTUS. *(Courtesy of Director of Antiquities).*

Above: Scene showing GANYMEDE taken away by Zeus disguised as an eagle. *(Courtesy of Director of Antiquities).*

bove: PENEUS — APOLLO and fascinating DAPHNE — another Love Story. *(Courtesy of Director of Antiquities).*

Phaedra and Hippolytos

This scene shows Hippolytos, the son of Theseus and the Amazon Queen Hippolyta. Theseus married Phaedra, daughter of Minos (Crete) but Phaedra fell madly in love with Hippolytos who was her son. When he did not respond to her advances she got cross and to hurt him accused him of trying to seduce her. She then killed herself.

His father believed Phaedra and to punish his son, asked Poseidon's assistance. He sent a sea monster which frightened Hippolytos' horse, he fell and died. Theseus discovered the truth but the tragedy had already occurred.

The scene shows Hippolytos ignoring Phaedra and to the right Eros.

Ganymedes

A beautiful scene surrounded with equally beautiful patterns. Here, Zeus, transformed into an eagle, kidnaps Ganymedes and carries him away.

According to the mythology, the daughter of Zeus Hebe and Hera who was also the Goddess of Youth stumbled and fell down when serving the Gods.

For failing in her duties she was expelled from her office, in order to replace the cup-bearer. Zeus took a fancy to the beautiful young Ganymedes when he was playing with Cupid. He transformed himself into an eagle and abducted him to Mount Olympus.

The Peacock

A beautiful small scene showing a peacock displaying its colourful feathers.

Other interesting scenes include:

The Four Seasons — Narcissus — Poseidon and Anemone — Hunting scenes, mosaic scenes filled with vine loaded with grapes plus geometric patterns.

A very comprehensive and detailed description of the House of Dionysos and the various mosaic scenes has been written by Professor G.S. Eliades, owner of the Ethnographic Museum at 1 Exo Vrisis Street, Paphos.

(15) THE HOUSE OF THESEUS

The excavations here cover a wide area and have been going on since 1965 under the direction of the Polish archaeologist W.A. Daszewski. Due to its size and importance it is believed to be the residence of the Roman Governor. Over 100 rooms and corridors have been unearthed. Many floors had mosaics, most with geometric patterns some of which survive but the most important are:

Theseus and the Minotaur

An extremely fine mosaic, one of the best in the Roman world. It has a large, circular patterned panel and in the middle is a scene with the figure of Theseus ready to hit the minotaur with a club. Above him in the upper part, is the personification of Crete and Ariadne. Lower, to the left is a figure of an old man symbolising the Labyrinth.

The Bath of Achilles

A long panel in the main hall of the villa. In the centre of the mosaic shows Thetis lying on a couch. She has just given birth to Achilles; to the left is Anatrophe (the nurse) holding Achilles and she prepares him for his first bath. Behind her is the servant girl Ambrosia.

To the right is Peleus, Achilles' father; behind him, on the right, are the Three Fates. First is Clotho, Lachesis and Anthropos carrying a scroll whereon is written their destiny for Achilles. This particular mosaic is believed to be of the early 5th century AD.

Other smaller mosaics include Neptune and Amphitrite.

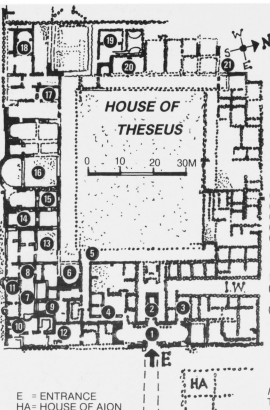

HOUSE OF THESEUS

0   10   20   30M

EAST WING
(1) MAIN ENTRANCE
Large room with mosaic floor with geometric patterns.
(2) Main ATRIUM — Similar to those of Pompeii & Herculaneum.
(3) & (4) DWELLING AREAS.
(5) Fine Geometric Floor.

SOUTH WING
(6) THE THESEUS MOSAIC Floor — a stately room of recreational character.
(7) Luxurious BATH Complex.
(8) COLD ROOMS decorated with a fine geometric mosaic.
(9) Two large BASINS.
(10) OVEN generating Heat.
(11) STEAM Bathroom.
(12) LATRINE room for 12-14 people.
(13) — (15) CHAMPERS.
(16) ACHILLES MOSAIC
— Main hall & horseshoe shaped apse.

WEST WING
(17) — (19) Various CHAMPERS for residence & storage.
(20) & (21) In these two rooms many marble statues of Gods and Goddesses were found, most of the 2-3rd cent AD. These finds include Aphrodite, Dionysos, Artemis, Asklepeion, Isis; all on display at Paphos Museum.

NORTH WING
This was for the servants, slaves and also was used as a laundry and workshop area.

E = ENTRANCE
HA = HOUSE OF AION

Mosaic representing the bath of Achilles from the House of Theseus. *(Courtesy of Director of Antiquities)*

43

Above: Remains of the House of Theseus. *Below:* Impressive scene of .Theseus slaying the Minotaur. *(Courtesy, Director of Antiquities).*

(16) THE HOUSE OF AION (or AEON)

This is a new addition to the above two houses and is between them (nearer to the House of Theseus), to the east side. It was discovered in 1983 by W.A. Daszewski. Only part of the house has been excavated and the mosaic floors found here are of excellent quality. After careful restoration they have been covered now into a room with the help of the Leventis foundation. The scenes are divided into 5 panels of which four are smaller. They are believed to belong to the 4th century AD.

Panel (A) — The Presentation of Baby Dionysos

Sitting Hermes presents baby Dionysos to Tropheus who is surrounded with the Nymphs. Other figures to the left are Anatrophe and further left Nysa. Behind Hermes are Ambrosia and Nectar and to the right is Theogonia (Birth of Gods).

Panel (B) — Leda & the Swan

It shows Leda in the centre ready to take a bath in the river Eurotas. Disguised as a swan, Zeus is surrounded with 3 young women, the Lacedaemonians. Unfortunately this has been badly damaged.

Panel (C) — A Beauty Contest between Cassiopi & Nereids

Divided into two panels, this long mosaic

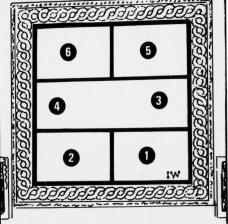

(1) Panel (A) Presentation of Dionysos.
(2) Panel (B) Leda & the Swan
(3 & 4) Panel C Beauty Contest between Cassiopi and Nereids.
(5) Panel (D) Apollo & Marsyas.
(6) Panel (E) Triumphant procession of baby Dionysos.

has, in the middle, the damaged figure of AION. To his right he points at Cassiopi, queen of Ethiopia; the winner — who is about to be crowned by Krisis.

To the right hand of the panel are the loosers, the Nereids — Doris, Thetis and Galatea, carried away into the sea by Bithos and Pontos; on the upper part of both

Part of the panel showing the Nereids during the contest with Cassiopi. (Cour.esy, Director of Antiquities).

panels are other figures such as Helios (left) Zeus and Athena (right).

Olympus (his son) is begging for mercy.

Panel (D) — Apollo & Marsyas

A musical contest with Marsyas daring to compete with Apollo. For this he was skinned alive. Here, he is carried by two Scythians to the place of punishment.

Panel (E) — The Triumphant Procession of Baby Dionysos

Many figures including that of Dionysos have been damaged. He is on a chariot led by a pair of centaurs. The procession is led by a young woman holding a quiver.

Above: The Presentation of Baby Dionysos. *Below:* Beautiful Leda on the Swan (badly damaged) — House of Aion. *(Courtesy, Director of Antiquities).*

(17) HOUSE OF ORPHEUS

A panel depicting Hercules and the Lion was originally discovered in 1943 by British soldiers who were camped here. It was then covered up. Excavations of the area started in 1982 under Dr. D. Michaelides. The scene of Hercules originally gave the name as the House of Hercules. When the larger and most impressive mosaic of Orpheus and the Animals was discovered the name was changed to the House of Orpheus. Excavations continue in the surrounding area. The mosaics have been restored with the assistance of the Getty Foundation and they will be opened to the public shortly.

The Main Panel –

ORPHEUS AND THE BEASTS

Orpheus sitting on a rock plays his Lyre. Various birds, animals and beasts have gathered around him. Orpheus' musical abilities were such that even trees and stones would respond. The inscription above his head gives the name of the owner of the house as Titus Restitutus.

Hercules & the Lion

The first panel to be discovered; this depicts Hercules' first Labour — the fight with the Lion of Nemea. After a long struggle, Hercules kills the animal with his bare hands, which is shown on the mosaic.

An Amazon

A small panel just above that of Hercules. It shows an Amazon — war loving daughters of Mars — standing beside her horse carrying her double axe. This is an unusual scene.

Orpheus and the Beasts, House of Orpheus. *(Courtesy, Director of Antiquities).*

(18) FABRICA HILL

This hill lies at the entrance to Kato Paphos village, along the main road from the town of Paphos (Ktima), and forms the north east limits of the ancient city walls. These rocks are interesting due to several underground rock-cut caves and chambers. Some of the caves have vaulted roofs and plastered walls, which may have been painted. Some are large. They date back to the Hellenistic period, as far as the 3rd Century BC. No clear evidence exists as to the purpose of the chambers. The public is free to visit them at any time, but take care in case loose rocks fall. It is unfortunate that on the western side and to the west of the main road, hotel and apartment complexes have destroyed part of the city walls.

Above: Petra tou Dhigeni. *Below:* Entrance to Apollo Hylates Sanctuary.

(19) PETRA TOU DHIGENI (Dhigenis rock)

This rock (Petra tou Dhigeni), which lies on another smaller rock in a most peculiar way, is situated to the north of Fabrica Hill and has a very interesting legend attached to it. There was once a medieval Greek hero called Dhigenis who had tremendous physical power.

During his stay in Cyprus he visited the Queen of Paphos, Rhigena, and fell in love with her beauty. The town of Paphos was suffering from a shortage of water and the Queen asked Dhigenis to bring water from the mountain and, if he succeeded, she would marry him. After much hard work Dhigenis managed to succeed with the task, only to discover that Queen Rhigena had changed her mind. In his anger he ran up the hill of Moutallos overlooking the kingdom of Paphos and, with his powerful little finger, he threw the rock at the Queen. He failed to hit her and she, in turn, threw her distaff at him, but missed her target. Eventually they got together and lived as a couple near the cave of Ayios Agapetikos.

(20) THE THEATRE

The Theatre lies to the south east of Fabrica Hill and is still covered with earth. Plans are made for future excavation and restoration. The Theatre was built in a commanding position, with a good view of the sea and town. According to a Hellenistic inscription found in the area the date of the Theatre is thought to be the 3rd Century BC.

(21) SANCTUARY OF APOLLO HYLATES

These rock-cut underground chambers which lie south east of the East Gate and north of Paphos Beach Hotel, are the sanctuary of Apollo Hylates. Inscriptions are to be seen in Cypro-Syllabic script cut above the entrance, which explain that the cave is dedicated to Apollo Hylates by the High Priest Dajaphas the Ajaros. The caves date back to the 4th Century BC. For many years the sanctuary, which stands amongst pine and cypress trees, was a sacred spot. The sanctuary is situated on private property but when the area was visited by the author, the gate was open and rfo one was around. Should you have any problem in getting to the sanctuary, please contact the museum for advice.

(22) THE EASTERN NEKROPOLIS
This has come to light during recent excavations. It covers an area between the Annabelle and Alexander the Great hotels and over the other side of the main road. During recent works for the construction of hotels and shops many tombs were discovered and explored by the Museum of Paphos. Those of greater importance have been preserved and incorporated within the above mentioned hotels.

(23) BYZANTINE CASTLE
Overlooking the harbour stands the castle which, it is believed, dates back to the 7th Century AD and was built in order to protect the port and town against the Arab raids. The locals also call it "Saranta

Ruins in the Kato Paphos old town. Most of the old buildings are under the foundations of new houses.

Fabrica Hill rock formations and caves by the main road.

Kolones" (forty columns), because of the number of broken granite columns found lying around.

Recent excavations have revealed more of the castle, the walls, the various quarters and rooms, courtyards and underground chambers. It is open to the public at all times and the visitor is requested to take great care to avoid any damage. When Richard The Lion Heart occupied Cyprus in 1191 AD the castle surrendered to him, but eventually it was destroyed by an earthquake in 1222 AD.

The castle had eight towers of different shapes defending the thick outer walls. Part of the castle has been restored, and gives some impression of its original size. Once it was believed to be the site of a Temple of Aphrodite but excavation discovered the castle, a very important monument to visit and explore.

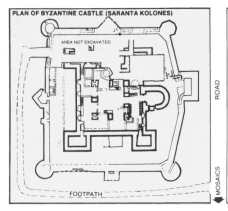

Plan of the Byzantine Castle of Saranta Kolones.

Below and *far right:* Two views of the partly restored Byzantine Castle.

(24) THE ODEON

Excavated and now restored, the Odeon is one of the most impressive monuments of Paphos. In the summer local professional theatre companies perform ancient Greek plays and it is worth enquiring at your hotel for the dates. The first play was performed on 29th June 1975 by local students. The play was MEDEA by Euripides was directed by C. Kakoyiannis. The Odeon was built entirely of stone with a semi-circular orchestra around the 2nd Century AD. Originally it had 25 tiers and seated 3000 people. It can now accommodate up to 1200 people.

(25) THE AGORA

Dated at the same period as the Odeon the Agora stands in front of the Theatre. It has been partially excavated and only foundations can be seen, with some granite columns lying on the ground. The Agora was used mainly for shopping and gatherings. Most of it is now covered with grass and soil and it is difficult to imagine how important it once was.

(26) THE ASKLEPEION

Next to the Odeon is the Asklepeion building where more can be seen than in the Agora. It consists of three parts of corridors, large rooms and some unspoilt chambers. Excavations are continuing on this site. The Asklepeion, the only one found in Cyprus, was dedicated to the God of Medicine and Healing — ASKLE-PEIOS. As a God he could heal practically anything and he was helped by special powers such as from snakes and his four daughters: HYGIA (Health); IASSO (Therapy); EGLI (The Bright One) and PANAYIA (All Cure).

The Asklepeion was the Temple and the place where the God was worshipped. It was also the place for treatment and used as a school for teaching. Doctors performed cures after following a strict programme of internal and external cleansing.

(27) THE AKROPOLIS (LIGHTHOUSE)

There can be no ancient city without the Akropolis (the highest rock spot where a temple always stood) and Paphos is no exception. Unfortunately no temple exists now but some remains of the Hellenistic and Roman periods have recently been found. On the rock now stands a lighthouse and some houses, which make an interesting complex. Rock-cut steps can be seen on the side of the Odeon leading down from the Akropolis to the Theatre.

The lighthouse which is built over the ancient Akropolis.

Above: The restored Odeon. On the foregound granite columns are the remains of the Agora.
Below: An ancient Greek Comedy performed at the Odeon.

(28) AMPHITHEATRE
Behind the Castle and the Customs House used to lie the Amphitheatre. All that is visible now is the oval-shaped depression in the ground. Some foundations were discovered but practically everything surviving is still buried.

(29) THE CITY WALLS
(Northwest Gate)
The City Wall which surrounded the town as shown on the map has been more or less destroyed. Some traces can be seen around Fabrica Hill, but most important are those behind the lighthouse (Akropolis). At this point the wall followed the edge of the rocky cliffs, which protected it from the sea. The North West gate which lies here was cut from the rock and one can see the remains of a bridge by this gate. Excavations are under way which may throw more light on the old defences of the town and part of it that has been cleared is an interesting place to view.

(30) GARRISON'S CAMP
More complex underground rock-cut caves can be seen near Ayios Lambrianos, most of them still to be excavated. They resemble the Apollo Sanctuary but there is no evidence to justify this identification positively. The date of origin is believed to be the 4th Century BC and it is widely held that this area was used as a main base for various armies as a camp, including the Egyptian Ptolemaic troops and the Romans.

(31) PAINTED TOMBS
These tombs were discovered recently whilst some construction was under way. They are to remain open for the public to view. They are close to the Garrison Camp rocks. The walls and ceilings of both tombs were painted with flora and geometric patterns. The two tombs date back to the Hellenistic period and it is believed that they were also used at later dates. Some tombs are on the southern side of Tombs of Kings Avenue surrounded by flats.

(32) FRANKISH BATHS
This small, medieval building with a domed roof is situated close to the Sofi-Anna apartments.
It was built during the Lusignan period and was then used over the years as public baths accommodating over 100 people daily.

The remains of the Frankish Baths.

Excavations take place slowly but systematically in ancient Paphos.

Above: Remains of the City Walls (Northern Gate) fortifications.
Below: Rock Cut chambers at the Garrison's Camp area.

KATO PAPHOS

TO: CORAL BAY
AYIOS YEORYIOS PEYIAS
AKAMAS/POLIS

PLOUTARCHOU

ST. PAULS AVENUE

K. NICOLAOU

LIDAS ST.

POSEIDONOS AVE.

PAFIA
APHRODITE

(P)

SCALE:
0 .... 500 METR
0 .... 1/4 ...... MILE

(1) THE HARBOUR
(2) MEDIEVAL CASTLE
(3) PANAYIA LIMENIOTISSA
(4) LATIN CATHEDRAL
(5) EARLY CHRISTIAN BASILICA
(6) ST. PAUL'S PILLAR
(7) GOTHIC CHURCH
(8) AYIA KYRIAKI CHURCH
(9) PANAYIA THEOSKEPASTI
(10) ST. ANTONY'S CHURCH
(11) AYIA SOLOMONI
(12) AYIOS LAMBRIANOS
(13) AYIOS AGAPITIKOS
(14) HOUSE OF DIONYSOS
(15) HOUSE OF THESEUS
(16) HOUSE OF AION
(17) HOUSE OF ORPHEUS
(18) FABRICA HILL
(19) DHIGENIS ROCK
(20) THEATRE
(21) SANCTUARY OF APOLLO
(22) EASTERN NEKROPOLIS
(23) BYZANTINE CASTLE

(24) THE ODEON
(25) AGORA
(26) ASKLEPEION
(27) AKROPOLIS
(28) AMPHITHEATRE
(29) CITY WALLS
(30) GARISSON'S CAMP
(31) PAINTED TOMBS
(32) FRANKISH BATHS
(33) TOMBS OF KINGS
      (see Map of KTIMA/PAPHOS)
(34) ART GALLERY
(35) POST OFFICE

(36) CYDIVE CLUB
(37) SODAP WINERY
(38) PUBLIC BEACHES
(39) TO YEROSKIPOS BEACH (PLAZ)
      CHILDREN'S PLAYGROUND
      SAILING CLUB
      TENNIS CLUB
(40) GOVERNMENT OFFICES
(P) PARKING
(S) SCHOOL

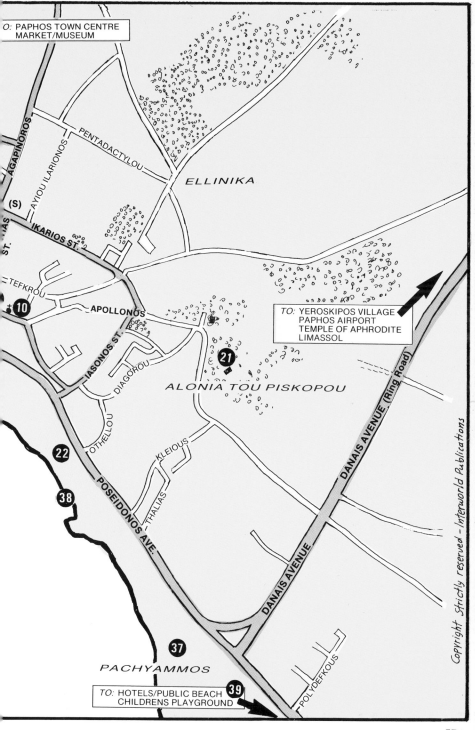

O: PAPHOS TOWN CENTRE
MARKET/MUSEUM

AGAPINOROS

ST. HAS

(S)

AYIOU ILARIONOS

PENTADACTYLOU

ELLINIKA

IKARIOS ST.

TEFKROU

10

APOLLONOS

IASONOS ST.

DIAGOROU

21

ALONIA TOU PISKOPOU

TO: YEROSKIPOS VILLAGE
PAPHOS AIRPORT
TEMPLE OF APHRODITE
LIMASSOL

DANAIS AVENUE (Ring Road)

OTHELLOU

22

KLEIOUS

POSEIDONOS AVE.

THALIAS

38

DANAIS AVENUE

37

PACHYAMMOS

TO: HOTELS/PUBLIC BEACH
CHILDRENS PLAYGROUND

39

POLYDEFKOUS

(33) TOMBS OF THE KINGS

These rock-cut tombs, unique of their type in Cyprus, are situated north west of the town of Kato Paphos and form an impressive Necropolis with caves, chambers, fascinating rock formations and tombs. Most of the area is still covered and is to be excavated.

The tombs, with heavy Doric-style columns and chambers cut in the rock below ground level, were used as a burial ground in the Hellenistic period (3rd Century BC) and later by the Romans. During the Christian persecutions by the Romans some tombs were used as a refuge.

They were further used during Medieval times and some changes were made. Severe looting occurred at various times which caused the destruction of many important items. The site was also used as a quarry, thus inflicting even more damage to the tombs. Excavations were carried out between 1937 and 1951 but, due to the lack of professional and scholarly supervision, practically all the evidence discovered was then lost. Very careful and systematic excavations are being carried out at present and new types of tombs have been discovered. However, a tour of the Necropolis is a must for every visitor, archaeology lover or not, since it combines a unique beauty with a natural and fascinating setting. Although the tombs are called Tombs of The Kings, no evidence has yet been found that they were used for the burial of Royalty.

Excavations continue under the direction of Savvas Hadjisavvas and new tombs and important items come to life from time to time such as that uncovered in 1988 in the central section which to the surprise of many was intact. It was of the Hellenistic period and many Ptolemaic coins, lamps, and other items were found.

Above and *right:* Two different types of tombs presenting their unique fascination and glory.

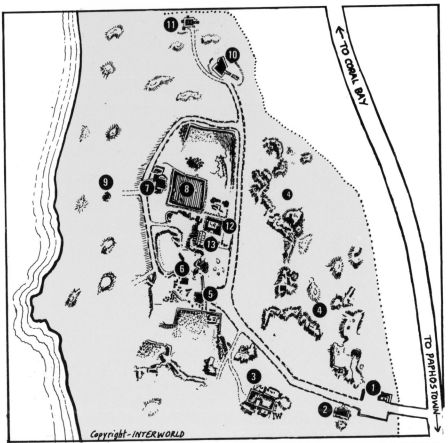

TOMBS OF KINGS

(1) Entrance & Car Park
(2) MONOPORTI TOMB
(3) TUMULUS —
    "Paleokastra" cemetery
(4) Rock Formations
(5) Peristyle Atrium Tomb
    Complex
(6) Peristyle Atrium 2nd
    Tomb Complex
(7) Pillaster — Atrium
    Tomb Complex
(8) Open Yard
(9) Well
(10) Complex of 3 Tombs
(11) Palioeklishia Peristyle
    Tomb
(12) Ptolemaic Tomb
(13) Horse Skeleton

Above: Location plan of
the area of the Tombs.
Left: Another type of
tomb.

MODERN PAPHOS

In all, while many parts of the ancient city of NEA PAPHOS are under modern houses, hotels and shops, a great part of it has been preserved and occupies the western side of Apostolos Pavlos Avenue. It includes the area behind the shops up to the harbour and beyond along the coast to the North West Gate and up to the Painted Tombs. This land, which includes the Odeon, the Mosaics etc has been purchased by the Department of Antiquities and is under the patronage of UNESCO as an ancient city.

Modern Paphos built over the last few years, partly over the ancient city is a small but cosmopolitan tourist resort which has a relaxed, comfortable atmosphere.

Above: Relaxing on the beach. *Right:* Romantic view from Paphos Beach hotel. *Below:* The beach in front of Alexander the Great Hotel.

Above: Shopping street in Kato Paphos close to the sea.
Below: A romantic sunset as seen every night in front of the hotels on the side of the sea.

CHAPTER 3

EXPLORING THE COUNTRYSIDE

With this Guide you can explore the parts of Paphos you wish to see and by the route, the way you prefer. If you don't have a car, you can arrange to hire a taxi for a day. The taxi driver will either take you and leave you at your destination and return to pick you up in the evening, or he will drive you around.

Even if you are staying in other parts of Cyprus such as Limassol, visiting some places in Paphos is a must, and please remember, it takes only about an hour to drive from Limassol to Paphos town. Some tourist companies and tourist agencies offer tours to the most popular places. You can contact them for information.

The beautiful Paphos district offers a bit for everybody, the beaches of Coral Bay or Chrysochou Bay or Aphrodites Baths, the mountains, the villages, the monasteries.

Hoggarth wrote the following in his book DEVIA CYPRIA in 1887-88 when he visited Paphos and explored the countryside.

"Nature has defined it so clearly that we can hardly mistake the boundaries in spite of written authority. On the north and west lies the sea. Upon the east, the mass of Troodos continued in the rugged forest to Pomos Point, interposed a huge barrier between the west and the east of the island, which even under Evagoras, the Kingdom of Salamis appears not to have passed. At the northern end of this barrier, the kingdom of Paphos marched with that of Soloi. Lastly, upon the south, the tremendous cleft, cut by the Kostitheos river (a name not appearing in todays maps) up to mount Troodos, bounds the Kingdom of Curium . . . . "

PLEASE REMEMBER

If you drive, be careful, make sure that you have plenty of fuel (most petrol stations are closed on Saturday afternoons, Sundays and holidays). Check the tyres, take plenty of water and a torch for the night. Also take drinking water as the heat makes you thirsty. In the **KAFENION of the village** (the pub of Cyprus), which you cannot miss as it is always situated in the square, you will find refreshments. For eating if you are away from the main tourist areas it is advisable to take sandwiches etc., as you may not be able to find a place to have a cooked meal.

If you explore the countryside on foot, please take high boots with you for there is a rare chance you may disturb a snake, some are harmless but some are poisonous. Carry basic medical supplies and provisions for eating and drinking and if you plan to spend the night out, a sleeping bag.

Whether you are in the country or by the beach, do not expose your skin and head too much to the sun, especially during the first few days of your stay. Sun burns are very unpleasant and the sun is very strong.

VISITING OTHER PARTS OF CYPRUS

Although it is far to travel to **Ayia Napa**, you can go to **NICOSIA** in just over 2 hours and if you leave early in the morning you can be in the capital by 8 or 9am giving you plenty of time for a stroll around the shops or a visit to the **Cyprus Museum**, then return by late afternoon.

Or you can explore the **TROODOS** mountains and visit the best and largest monastery of Cyprus (**Kykko Monastery**) although avoid such a journey around 14-16 August when all the locals drive there for a festival.

You can visit the famous **TEMPLE OF APOLLO HYLATES** and the ancient city of **CURIUM** with its beautiful theatre. Further away towards Limassol is **KOLOSSI CASTLE** with its fascinating medieval architecture. And **Limassol** town is only just over an hours drive from Paphos.

IN THE FOOTSTEPS OF APHRODITE

The route from Paphos to Petra tou Romiou (the famous birthplace of Aphrodite) demands careful driving and observation of the road signs, since this is the very busy main road between Paphos and Limassol. Always remember to take extra care. However, it is a very pleasant trip, passing through green fields of banana, citrus trees, vines and peanuts — the only place in Cyprus where they are grown. The airport of Paphos, which is now fully operational, is on the south of the road close to the sea, near Akhelia. The journey to Petra tou Romiou is 16 miles, but various stops should be made to explore important places of interest.

ROUTE A-1 – **TO PALEAPAPHOS**

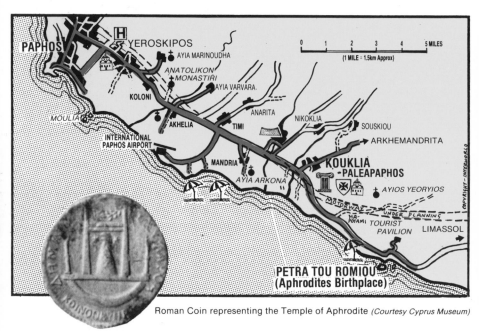

Roman Coin representing the Temple of Aphrodite *(Courtesy Cyprus Museum)*

YEROSKIPOS

This village is so close to the main town of Paphos they are almost joined together. The worship of Aphrodite brought great importance to this small place. Here were her Holy Gardens (Yieros Kipos) where pilgrims, after disembarking at the port of Paphos, stopped to relax before continuing their journey to the Holy Temple of Paleapaphos. The village square, with cafes and souvenir shops, is always busy with people. Strolling along to the south of the square you will reach **Ayia Paraskevi Church**. This church was built in the 11th Century AD and has five domes. The interior is also very interesting with some

fine wall paintings depicting scenes such as The Resurrection of Lazarus, The Entrance into Jerusalem, The Last Supper and many others. There are also some beautiful icons for the visitor to see.

Another place that one should not miss is the **Folk Art Museum** which is open daily. Between 1799 and 1864 this house was the British Consulate for the area. It is called the Haji Smith House. A Greek immigrant from the Greek island of Kephalonia, Andreas Zamboulaki, was appointed by Sir Sidney Smith, after his victory over Napoleon's army in Egypt. The appointment took place in 1799 and Andreas Zamboulaki, now as a British

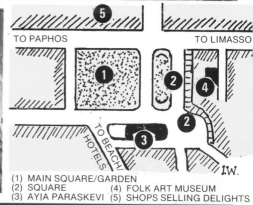

```
                                          5
TO PAPHOS                                      TO LIMASSO

                    1              2        4

                                        2
        TO BEACH
        HOTELS          3
                                              I.W.
```

(1) MAIN SQUARE/GARDEN
(2) SQUARE   (4) FOLK ART MUSEUM
(3) AYIA PARASKEVI   (5) SHOPS SELLING DELIGHTS

Above Top: The church of Ayia Paraskevi with its five domes.
Above: One of the many frescoes of the church "The Washing of the Feet" (15th cent.)
(Courtesy Cyprus Museum).
Right: The main square of Yeroskipos. Is surrounded by shops, tavernas and kafenia.

65

THE YEROSKIPOS DELIGHTS

No visitor to Yeroskipos will miss the numerous stalls on both sides of the road selling this traditional local product of "LOUKOUMIA" – Turkish Delights. The original industry was established in 1895 but the man who produced such excellent ingredients took his secret to the grave. There are now different brands with their own distinctive taste. Ideal purchase for your home or as a gift to friends.

The Folk Art Museum, an old house with a fine collection of various interesting objects.

Consular Agent, had the job of providing the British fleet with fresh supplies and provisions when they visited Paphos. The house has interesting architectural points and is now well preserved as a Folk Art Museum. There are various items on display such as costumes, tools, wood carvings, embroidery, household items and so on.

KOLONI

This is a small village. In the past however, its soil produced earth of different colours "Terra d'umbra" which was ideal for pottery. It is here that Savvas a refugee from Kyrenia, and his family have set up a pottery workshop. It has become one of the best modern Cypriot potteries. You are free to explore the workshops.

ANATOLIKON MONASTERY

This building, once functioning as a monastery, is now a farmhouse and acts as a centre for the surrounding farms. The medieval church of *Ayios Charalambos* is most intriguing and worth a visit.

AKHELIA

An important agricultural centre, situated by the side of the river Ezousas south of the main road. It is widely believed that the area was inhabited by ancient Greeks and Romans and during medieval times it became a major sugar producing centre and also a Commandery (a feudal adminis-

trative district), under the Knights Hospitallers. Later it was owned by the Venetian firm of Martoni (1450 AD). Under the Turks it continued as an agricultural centre called *"Akhelia Chiftlik"*. Now it is a very important agricultural station.

There are two interesting churches. *Ayios Theodosios* is pretty and of a unique Byzantine style (only four of this design exist in Cyprus). The altar contains some Roman marble. *Ayios Yeoryios* is a medieval church. There were some remarkable woodcarvings and other objects which were removed and sold in auctions in London around 1900. Only a few icons now remain.

TIMI *(see route B-4)*

The Paphos International Airport

Nicely situated, close to the sea and south of Akhelia and Timi, this new ultra-modern airport also possesses a long runway suitable for the biggest jets. It started official direct flights to the U.K., Greece and other places for tourist traffic in April 1984. Every year a small number of extra flights are added as the demand for visiting Paphos from various parts of Europe is increasing. It is also used for transporting agricultural products.

The Church of Ayios Theodosios — Akhelia.

MANDRIA

An agricultural centre south of the main road with some 400 inhabitants. There is a church that is worth a visit with a strange marble capital and a female head above the west door. To the south east of the village there is a small chapel, *Ayia Arkona,* built on top of an ancient site.

Further south, near the sea there are further remains of old ruins, some possibly submerged under water. It is worth noting that to the north east of this area is Paleapaphos and it is believed that a small harbour was in operation from cape Zephyros and along the eastern coast.

There is an old quarry in the area and also some strange **MONOLITHS,** the largest of which is about 10 feet high above ground and pierced with holes. Similar types of stones are to be found in some other parts of Paphos and Cyprus. Although one simple theory is that they were used as oil mills, they are still surrounded with mystery.

Above Right: The mysterious monoliths. Recent excavations indicate their origin from the Hellenistic period and believed to have been used for making oil. *(Photo: Stephanos Theodorou).*
Below: An old engraving of Paleapaphos.

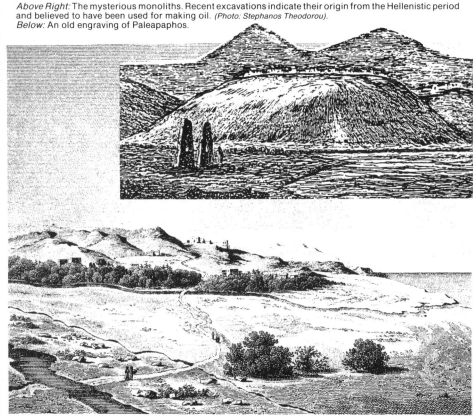

THE ANCIENT KINGDOM OF PALEAPAPHOS
& The Temple of Aphrodite

Remains of the Temple of Aphrodite believed to be dated to around 1200BC.

KOUKLIA (PALEAPAPHOS)

The highlight of this particular trip is the visit to this once very famous place, Kouklia. This was the centre for the worship of Aphrodite and pilgrims came here from all over the Mediterranean. Make sure you do not miss the turning (to the left as you come from Paphos) since it is on a bend, though it is well sign-posted.

The old town was situated in a commanding position on a flat-topped hill overlooking the valley and the sea, which is about one mile to the south. The view from the top is excellent. The town of Kouklia was established by Agapenor, King of Tegea (Arcadia — Greece). There is evidence though from recently discovered tombs around the area that a settlement was established there much earlier and some

form of worship was already in progress. The legend says that Pygmalion, one of the kings of the town, was also a good sculptor and carved many statues. Eventually he fell passionately in love with one of them, so much so that Aphrodite decided to turn the statue into a real woman and gave it life. From this relationship was born a son, Paphos, thus giving his name to the Town. However, the most famous man of Palea-paphos was Kinyras, who is believed to have been the major influence behind the newly-emerged Cypriot civilisation. Under his direction there were many new inventions using metals, and he also placed a lot of emphasis on music and musical instruments. As the High Priest of the Temple he introduced further mysteries into the religious festivities, most of which he brought from Egypt.

69

BRIEF HISTORY OF PALEAPAPHOS

The first archaeological excavations started at Kouklia by Joseph Hammer Von Purgstall in 1800 but without much success. This was followed by Luigi Palma de Cesnola between 1869-70 who inflicted much damage.

In 1888-89 the Cyprus Exploration Fund set up by the new British administration started preliminary excavations at the Temple site and also discovered various tombs nearby.

In 1950 the second British expedition started work in and around Kouklia and work by various foreign groups and the Department of Antiquities has continued ever since. The latest finds are of the medieval period, the sugar cane refining installations.

Below we document a very brief chronology of the history of PALEAPAPHOS. For those who would like more detailed information which also includes Nea Paphos, we highly recommend the book by F.G. Maier & V. Karageorgis, **"Paphos-History and Archaeology"**.

CHALCOLITHIC PERIOD c.2800BC.
Finds at Asproyi and Evreti areas show that some habitation existed during that period.

LATE BRONZE AGE 1650-1050BC.
Kinyras was the founder King of the pre-Greek population although the exact date is unknown. Finds at various tombs to the east of the town date to various periods of this age.

The **Greek Achaeans** settled here in the 12th century and assumed their role in the city although the Kinyrad dynasty continued as Rulers and High Priests for many hundreds of years.

The first sanctuary, it was believed, was established c.1200BC although its origins are shrouded in mystery.

The 11th century was a big turning point when the Greek settlers assumed their dominant role upon the city, mainly in culture and commerce as the Temple continued with an Eastern influence.

CYPRO-GEOMETRIC PERIOD
1050-750BC. This period is not very well documented and is regarded as the "dark ages".

ARCHAIC PERIOD 750-475BC. A
new revival. The city saw expansion. Fortifications were erected as from the 8th century. Although few remains of buildings were found, the tombs and graves revealed rich finds.

The Kinyrad family continued to rule as Kings and the High Priests of **WANASSA** (The Lady) as Aphrodite were the centre of the annual activity of the city and included also great cultural events. Homer wrote his *"Hymn to Aphrodite"* describing such events.

Syllabic script was developed and widely used. Coins wsere minted. Despite foreign occupation by Assyrians and Egyptians, the kingdom had a great degree of Independence.

The Persians occupied Cyprus in 545; the kingdom of Paleapaphos continued with its religious and political freedom.

THE SIEGE OF PALEAPAPHOS

In 499BC the *"Ionian Revolt"* in Asia Minor and Cyprus started against Persian rule. Paleapaphos strengthened its defences in anticipation of Persian attacks, but the Persian armies defeated the Greeks. In Cyprus, the Phoenician elements and kingdoms sided with the Persians — this influenced the outcome. In quick succession the rebellious kingdoms of Cyprus were defeated. In Paleapaphos a long siege started in 498BC. A mound (a band of earth or stones) was built by the Persians on the *North East Gate - Marcello Hill*. Buildings, Temples and Statues outside the walls were destroyed and used for the building of the mound. Such fragments were recently discovered in large quantities including a fine head of a Priest King, a Bronze Helmet, hundreds of spear and arrow heads, limestone figures and inscriptions.

Tunnels were constructed by defenders to undermine the mound and they removed as much material as possible. The mining of such tunnels was formidable; they were then filled with wood, set alight and the mound collapsed.

However, despite the heroic defences, the superiority of the Persians succeeded in overrunning the town by storm; there is no knowledge of the final events — although the actual siege is well documented.

Archaeologists regard this site second only to Masada in Israel for the importance of engineering siege techniques.

CLASSICAL PERIOD 475-325BC.
Despite the harsh Persian rule, the Kinyrad Kings retained some influence and continued to mint their own coins. Recorded kings included *Penthylos* and *Timocharis*. At first the walls remained unattended, although large buildings were erected. The surviving PALACE at Hadji Abdullah area is a fine building believed to have housed either the king or the Persian governor.

Large limestone blocks were used for the walls.

Although no remains of the Classical Temple remain, the cult of Aphrodite continued and Paphos remained the centre of worship. Economic activity was booming. Paleapaphos, together with all the other Cypriot Kingdoms declared support and assistance to Alexander the Great in 331BC. This change of events affected the Kingdom of Paleapaphos more than any other in the island.

HELLENISTIC PERIOD 325-58BC.

The last king to serve at Paleapaphos was **NICOCLES.** In c.320BC he transferred the seat of government to Nea Paphos which was established as a port. He was an enterprising monarch who built temples and buildings in Nea Paphos but also strengthened the Sanctuary of Aphrodite and Paleapaphos retained its Reglious importance. Cyprus came under the domination of the Greek rulers of Egypt the PTOLEMIES who established Nea Paphos as their administrative centre of the island. The Kinyrad family continued their role as the High Priests of the sanctuary and a new lease of life was given by the new rulers. Queen Arsinoe, sister of Ptolemy Philadelphus was introduced by her brother into the cult.

ROMAN PERIOD 58BC-330AD —

Paleapaphos saw a change under the Romans. The cult of Aphrodite, goddess of Fertility, gradually changed to VENUS, goddess of Love. The mysteries gained more sexual and lustful connotations.

Paleapaphos became a very important religious centre attracting thousands of visitors annually from all over the Empire. Visitors continued to disembark at Nea Paphos harbour, crowned with myrtle and accompanied with music started a procession to the sanctuary. Events included games, music, dancing and poetry.

New buildings were erected and coins were minted showing the sanctuary with the conical stone, symbol of fertility. Emperor Titus recorded that he visited Paleapaphos in 69AD.

The earthquake of 15BC inflicted severe damage but eventually the sanctuary was rebuilt with funds provided by Emperor Augustus. Finds from tombs of the Roman period indicate that very wealthy Roman families lived and were buried here.

A mosaic floor was found in one Roman villa, that of LEDA. It was housed at the Kouklia museum, it was then stolen and found in Europe, brought back to Cyprus and now is on display at the Cyprus Museum. It shows beautiful Leda from the back teasing amorous Zeus who is disguised as a swan; a fine mosaic.

EARLY BYZANTINE PERIOD 330-641AD.

Christianity was a turning point

Detail of the site of the North East Gate — *Marcello Hill* and the siege mount. Most excavated work is now covered with grass. The area is fenced.

Above and *below:* Two views of the remains of the once formidable Temple, centre of worship to Aphrodite.

Above: The now restored medieval Manor, used as a Museum and living quarters of various archaeological expeditions. Below: Some exhibits of the Museum.

73

for the Roman Empire and also for Palea-paphos. The newly established church objected strongly to the continuity of the rites, although the cult strongly resisted any changes during the early years; it was finally outlawed by Emperor Theodosios in 391AD.

Neglect and nature destroyed the sanctuary after 14 centuries of continuous activity.

MEDIEVAL-FRANKISH RULE – It was not until the 12th century AD that Paleapaphos known as **COUVOUCLE** (KOUKLIA) attracted the Lusignan rulers — thanks to its surrounding fertile land. A Royal manor was built on the southern site of the Temple from which stones were used. Nearby, a small but interesting church, KATHOLIKI CHURCH, served the Latin community. Kouklia became the commercial centre of Paphos with the production and the refinery of SUGAR, an extremely important commodity in those days. Ruins of the sugar cane refinery were recently found south of the Manor and the main Paphos-Limassol road and excavation work continues.

Places of interest:

The Temple: The ruins, which cover a wide area, have not yet been restored and show nothing of the impressive buildings which once stood there. The existing ruins are thought to be those of the Roman Temple which was built on the foundations of the original. A detailed description of the Temple is given in the Official Guide which one may obtain from the Museum. Some other remains were found around the Palace.

The Lusignan Manor House: This is the medieval building at the far end of the Temple which, since its restoration, is the Museum and is very interesting to visit. The Manor House was called the Château de Covocle but this was later destroyed and rebuilt by the Turks and called a Turkish Chiftlik. It housed the landlord, who administered the cultivation of the land.

The Museum: This is housed within the Lusignan Manor House (Chiftlik). The museum, although small is interesting with items found in and around Kouklia, including the Sacred Stone from the sanctuary of the Temple.

This was taken to the Cyprus Museum in Nicosia but now has been restored as close as possible to its original site.

PLAN OF THE SANCTUARY OF APHRODITE
(based on C.100 AD)

(1) **SANCTUARY I** — The original sanctuary.
(2) **SANCTUARY II** — The new Roman sanctuary with an open court surrounded by buildings. West side destroyed completely.
(3) **NORTH HALL** — Limestone slap pavements were used and some survived.
(4) **NORTH STOA** — Parts of a damaged mosaic floor remain.
(5) **EAST WING** — Built in large limestone blocks consisting of several rectangular rooms.
(6) **SOUTH STOA** — A long hall without interior divisions.
(7) **THE HALL**
(8) **TEMENOS** — Incorporating large Late Bronze Age structures.

The Plan of the Temple of Aphrodite. Modifications and changes occured over different periods during the long time of worshipping which continued for over 1200 years.

New rooms of ther Manor which have been recently restored are to be used for more exhibits and the Grand Hall for exhibitions and seminars.

Leda & Kyknos (Swan): This excellent mosaic was found at the Roman *"House of Leda"* near the Temple. It shows beautiful Leda teasing amorous Zeus who is disguised as a Swan. The mosaic is exhibited at the Cyprus Museum.

A reproduction of the mosaic has been placed on the original site which is to the west of the Temple. A visitor can take the path, west of the entrance to the Temple to reach the house.

The Katholiki Church: This small, impressive church, close to the Temple ruins, has a small courtyard all round with

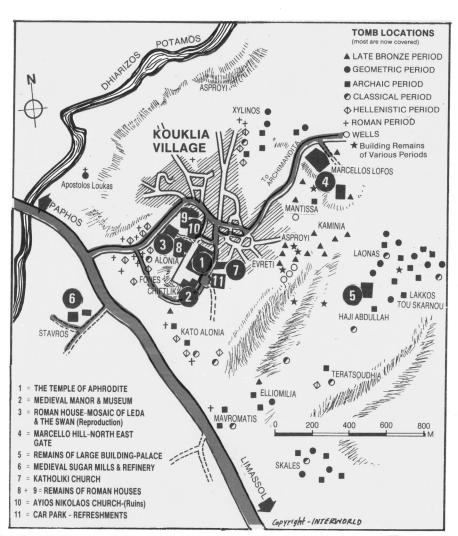

TOMB LOCATIONS
(most are now covered)

▲ LATE BRONZE PERIOD
● GEOMETRIC PERIOD
■ ARCHAIC PERIOD
◐ CLASSICAL PERIOD
◈ HELLENISTIC PERIOD
+ ROMAN PERIOD
○ WELLS
★ Building Remains of Various Periods

1 = THE TEMPLE OF APHRODITE
2 = MEDIEVAL MANOR & MUSEUM
3 = ROMAN HOUSE-MOSAIC OF LEDA & THE SWAN (Reproduction)
4 = MARCELLO HILL-NORTH EAST GATE
5 = REMAINS OF LARGE BUILDING-PALACE
6 = MEDIEVAL SUGAR MILLS & REFINERY
7 = KATHOLIKI CHURCH
8 + 9 = REMAINS OF ROMAN HOUSES
10 = AYIOS NIKOLAOS CHURCH-(Ruins)
11 = CAR PARK - REFRESHMENTS

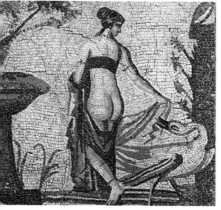

Left: LEDA and KYKNOS (Swan). This excellent Mosaic was found at the Roman House (3). It shows Leda teasing amorous Zeus — disguised as a swan. The original is in the Cyprus Museum (picture). A reproduction is exhibited on the site.
Right: Bronze helmet of the 5th cent. BC of Corinthian type found at the siege mount (4) now in the Cyprus Museum. *(Courtesy Cyprus Museum)*

Above: The now restored Katholiki Church, situated next to the Temple.
Left: Remains of the once busy medieval sugar mills — (see map).

columns and arches. The church dates from the 14th or 15th century and has interior frescoes and woodcarvings.

In the Village: In the square of the village we find the church of *Ayios Loukas.* Also some old houses are interesting.

Outside the Village: To the east and south east, along the valleys and the hills are some ancient tombs of various periods, most important being that of the *Spileon tis Regines.* To the west is a necropolis of the Bronze Age.

To the north **East Gate (site A)** on the side of Marcello Hill are to be seen the remnant of the siege works and the siege ramp (see page 34) and traces of the City Walls.

Further south of Hadji Abdullah **(site B)** are reamins of an important building which is said to have housed the Persian Commanders. Nearby are more signs of the city walls.

To the north, some 2 miles from the road to Arkhemandrita is a cave known as **Enklistra** of an unknown hermit with his tomb. Old frescoes are visible. Near the cave are the ruins of *St. Constantine* church and a monastery.

THE RITES OF APHRODITE and Adonis

Reconstruction drawing of the sanctuary of Aphrodite

As a religious centre, for the worship of the Goddess of Love, Paleapaphos attracted a great number of famous and influential people. In the Temple there was a granite stone — a sacred cone — which made Paleapaphos the centre of the world for the worshippers of Aphrodite.

During the festivals the cone was annointed with oil. The Priestesses of Love (the only people, apart from the High Priest, who were allowed access to the cone) would then dry it carefully with soft towels. No-one else was allowed to see the cone, which was regarded as sacred and covered with veils.

Various ceremonies took place over the year — The **Zakoria** probably the ceremony for the servants; The **Perioria** — before the main ceremonies and The **Aphrodisia.**

The Aphrodisia Festivities were an annual event and worshippers from all over the world would gather at Yeroskipos, in the Holy Gardens. From there they would follow the Holy Route towards Paleapaphos and the Temple. Many were spectators, but some were to take part in the four-day Mysteries.

During the first day sports and games were dedicated to the candidates.

THE SACRED CONE

This conical stone, found next to the Temple of Aphrodite by the English archaeologist J.L. Mayres in 1913 near the western end of the Roman South Stoa, is on show at Kouklia Museum — Paleapaphos.

Not large, only 1.22m in height, this Cult Idol of Aphrodite, a sacred stone, symbol of the **Goddess of Fertility and Love** provides an unsolved mystery. Such a stone cannot be found anywhere in the island and its origin is unknown. There is one theory that the stone is of a meteoric nature.

On the second day they bathed in the sea to the south of the town.

The third day was spent in the Temple with prayers and offerings of fruit, flowers and grain laid before the covered cone — the symbol of Aphrodite.

The final day of the Mysteries was the initiation. The worshipper gave the Priest a coin in exchange for a lump of salt. This exchange symbolised the birth of Aphrodite from the foam of the sea. The Priest then commenced the initiation, allowed the worshipper to enter into the Mysteries of Love by offering him a cake, and saying:

"Take this cake, symbol of the Goddess of Love and picture to yourself Aphrodite. Remember that her name is very sacred. You are not worthy even to mention it . . . she inspires . . ., she feeds you, me and everyone else . . ."

Together with the Mysteries and Rites of Aphrodite, another Festival also took place — that of the **Rites of Adonis.** Adonis, a handsome son of Kinyras and Metham, was the beloved youth of Aphrodite. But Adonis was loved not only by Aphrodite but also by Persephone, a beautiful but devilish Goddess of the underworld. Both being madly in love with Adonis, they continually quarrelled and fought each other. To put an end to this The *Court of The Gods* ruled that Adonis should give one third of his life per year to Aphrodite, one third to Persephone and keep one third for himself. However, he cheated and spent his own time with Aphrodite. When Persephone found out about this she was so furious and jealous that she decided to eliminate the man she so loved. One day Adonis while out hunting in the mountains of Paphos, came across Persephone. In her fury she turned a wild boar against him and he was killed. When Aphrodite heard the bad news she became hysterical. She ran through the woods to her dying lover cutting her legs, and from the blood of her injuries and her tears lilies started to grow . . . To Adonis' memory an annual funeral procession with mourners was held on the first day of the Rites and on the following day another ceremony depicted his resurrection. There were wild celebrations afterwards for the happy event.

Paphos (Paleapaphos) remained a religious centre for 16 Centuries, although the administration was moved to Nea Paphos during the Ptolemaic period; and during Roman times, which followed. The last King who ruled over the area of Paphos was Nicocles, who moved the administration of the new city of Nea Paphos towards the end of the 4th Century. The Temple was destroyed by one of the worst earthquakes in 15BC. The Roman Emperor Octavianus Augustus ordered its immediate restoration. The worshipping of Aphrodite and the rites were eventually put to an end by the Byzantine Emperors.

The Final death blow to this famous shrine of the Goddess Aphrodite was given by the decree of Emperor Theodosius (379-395AD) which closed down all pagan temples and prohibited any activity related to their worshipping.

Base of a Roman statue written in Greek with a dedication to Aphrodite Paphia found in the sanctuary.

THE PRIESTESSES OF APHRODITE IN ANCIENT PAPHOS

by *STASS PARASKOS*
Principal, Cyprus College of Art, Paphos

One of the most famous kings of ancient Cyprus was Cinyras who reigned in Paphos at the time of the Trojan War. He was a Phoenician prince who went to Cyprus with a band of followers seeking new homes because there was famine in their own country. They landed on the west coast of Cyprus near where the goddess Aphrodite had first set foot when she rose from the waves. The area was fertile and they were well content to settle there. So they built themselves a town, and in the centre of it erected a temple to Aphrodite, who, they believed, had guided them to her birthplace, and Cinyras became the first king and high priest of the new city, which they named Paphos in honour of his mother. For over a thousand years the Temple had remained a centre of worship and a meeting place for people of the Eastern Mediterranean; its fame ensuring that the goddess of Love would forever be associated with Paphos.

Cinyras had introduced sacred "prostitution" as part of the cult of Aphrodite and the temple in Paphos was famous for the large number of its beautiful priestesses. There were precedents for this, for in ancient times prostitution was a profession free of social or moral stigma. Indeed it was believed to fulfil social and educational needs and municipal brothels thrived throughout the ancient world. Many public figures, · including the great Athenian statesman Pericles were associated with prostitutes and the famous courtesan Phryne was commemorated with a statue at Delphi, the most sacred place in all Greece. The religious aspect of harlotry was based on the belief that anyone having intercourse with a priestess of the goddess of procreation would be rewarded with prosperity.

The priestesses of Aphrodite in Paphos, were trained in the complex rules of sacrifice, prayer and purification. They played prominent parts during the Aphrodisia festival and took part in sacrificial feasts. When public prayers were offered to the goddess their participation in large numbers was considered essential. Priestesses were not required to possess any special qualities other than the willingness to carry out their duties conscientiously. Some self-employed prostitutes worked part-time in the temple and were allowed to keep part of the money they had earned there.

The usual source of prospective priestesses was the lowest class of temple ministrants, called the sacred servants. Some of these servants were bought by the temple, others were dedicated to it by their parents when they were children. Their numbers ran into thousands of both sexes and all were at the high Priest's beck and call. Normally they would be put to domestic or agricultural work, but some of the women were creamed off and trained as priestesses.

Another source of priestesses were the wealthy pilgrims with their slave girls. In those times men always sought to gain the affection of their gods through bribery and to this effect the rich bought beautiful girls and dedicated them to Aphrodite. In return the goddess was expected to repay the kindness shown to her and for this reason, at the end of the dedication ceremony, the donors stood up with arms outstretched and palms turned expectantly upwards as though in the act of receiving a present.

All women in Paphos had to serve in the temple for one day a year during a festival called the Aphrodisia, celebrating the reunion of Aphrodite with her lover Adonis who returned from the dead at the beginning of every spring. The daughters of king Cinyras also served the goddess in this way — an indication that the rule embraced all women of a certain age, irrespective of social class. The girls wore special head scarves and sat in a line at the entrance of the great temple waiting to be chosen by a man. Men paraded up and down inspecting the girls and when one of them took their fancy they threw a silver coin in her lap and claimed her in the name of the goddess. The girls had no right to refuse a man and the silver coin went to the temple. The idea behind this rite was to imitate the reunion of Aphrodite with Adonis. For the same reason a sacred marriage between the High Priest, representing Adonis, and a priestess, representing Aphrodite, was performed in the Temple and was consummated in a chamber decorated with greenery. These rites pleased the goddess of fertility who responded by activating the creative forces of nature so that the crops grew and the animals were able to reproduce their kind.

In early antiquity, when women in Paphos were forbidden to marry unless they had first had intercourse with a stranger, all girls had to act as priestesses temporarily, until they were relieved of their maidenhood. In those days Cypriot men considered the act of deflowering a virgin dangerous and the temples of Aphrodite became crowded with girls waiting for foreign pilgrims. It is not surprising that some women waited for years before they attracted a lover.

It is wrong to assume that all the temples of Aphrodite were palaces of licence and debauchery and that all her priestesses were part-time prostitutes. It must be remembered that Aphrodite was not only the goddess of love but also the guardian of women in vulnerable positions, the protectress of innocence in young girls, she guarded over the sanctity of marriage and had powers to produce rain and calm the sea. There were temples dedicated to Aphrodite where the priestesses had to be virgins and if any of them broke her vows of chastity she was punished severely. On one occasion a priestess was buried alive. Men who accused a virgin priestess of Aphrodite without justification were charged before a priest-judge who could sentence them to have their foreheads branded.

The office of the high priest was not open to women but some priestesses, with special intuitive talents, rose to become oracles of the temple. These girls, being the main channel through which the goddess spoke, were extremely influential and were consulted by government officials and the military, as well as by private citizens. They spoke in the name of Aphrodite after having been stimulated by some device into an ecstatic condition. The knowledge that matters of life and death depended on their advice ensured that oracles would take their duties seriously. The vagueness of some of their answers was not designed merely to cover themselves in case of failure but was due also to their reluctance to commit themselves lightly. If one is to judge from their popularity, they seemed to have exercised their duties well and to the benefit of those who sought their advice.

Further reading
APHRODITE and the Mythology
of Cyprus
by STASS PARASKOS
is published by Interworld Publications
— Price UK £5.50 incl. postage.

Coins showing the Temple of Aphrodite (Roman Period).

80

PETRA TOU ROMIOU
(Aphrodite's Birthplace)

On reaching Petra tou Romiou (the Rock of the Greek) one can see impressive rock formations, with the largest rock close to the beach. Going up hill once passed the rock, you stop by the side of the road there is a beautiful view of the rock, the bay and the surrounding area. According to Greek mythology Aphrodite was born here. She rose from the white foam of the soft waves, floated on a sea shell and came to rest at Paleapaphos, where her Temple was erected.

In his Odyssey VIII, 362 Homer wrote:

"But laugher-loving Aphrodite went to Cyprus, to Paphos, in her precinct and fragrant altars . . ."
"The moist breeze of zephyr brought her there (to Paphos' shores) on the waves of the sea, with a noise of thunder, among the soft foam, and the gold-dressed Horä (beautiful women priestesses) received her with joy. They decked her with valuable jewels and on her immortal head they placed a beautiful gold crown and in her ears two earrings of copper and gold . . ."

For swimmers this is an ideal place, since the sea is usually very calm and the beach is sandy in places although on the eastern side there are pebbles. On the western side undercurrents occur and the water can get very deep. Nearby there is a restaurant and cafeteria run by the Tourist Organisation where one can eat and obtain refreshments. It is open all day and part of the night, and provides a wonderful view of the rock and the beach below. It is worth waiting here for the sunset which is beautiful.

Near the rocks more basic facilities provide car parking and minimal refreshments.

Sunset over the beautiful Petra tou Romiou where Aphrodite chose to come ashore.

Above: and *below:* Two different views of Aphrodite's Birthplace (Petra tou Romiou).

ROUTE A-2
TO ARKHIMANDRITA

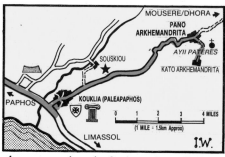

Some six to seven miles north east of Kouklia is the village of **Pano Arkhimandrita**. The drive is easy and the road wide, the scenery, like most other places in Paphos is constantly changing and breathtaking. The village is built at the top of a plateau and about ¾ of a mile below to the south is the old site of **Kato Arkhimandrita**. There are about 300 inhabitants in the village, mainly farmers, but like most of the villages, it has empty houses as people have emigrated to the towns or abroad. The village church has interesting icons of the 16th century in Cretan-Cypriote style.

Near Kato Arkhimandrita is the *Hermitage of Ayii Pateras* (Holy Fathers), it is inside a rock cut tomb believed to be of Roman origin. Some bones were kept in the cave in special places. A local story explains that the place is holy due to the slaughter of over 300 Christian refugees who came here from the persecutions in Syria, only to find an end to their lives from local people who objected to their presence.

For those with time on their hands and who like hard, slow driving in winding unsurfaced roads, further excursions to **Mousere** and **Dhora** (a village with an interesting church) will provide scenic views. After Dhora, the road is again good and for the return trip you go to Malia and from there either north to circle around Arsos —Ayios Nicolaos — Kedhares — Mamonia — Nikoklia or via Pakhna (going south), Prastio and Evdhimou.

Above: General view of Arkhimandrita village and
left: the entrance to Ayii Pateres cave.

83

ROUTE A-3
TO PISSOURI BAY

Although Pissouri is within the Limassol district, it is within the Paphos postal administration. A visit to the Bay can be enjoyed by everyone, as it offers good swimming and excellent eating.

Take the main road from Paphos to Limassol, pass Kouklia and the Birthplace of Aphrodite (Petra tou Romiou) and climb upwards and inland. Then you reach Pissouri. This is not the actual village which is ½ mile to the east on the side of the mountain. The cafes here were established many years ago as a stopping place when the road was very narrow and twisting and the journey took three times as long as now. Continuing along the main road down the valley on a straight stretch of the road you will see the signs for the Pissouri Columbia Beach Hotel to the right. Here you drive through one of the best vineyards of Cyprus which produces **Sultani Table Grapes.** Eventually you reach the Bay which is now a major tourist centre with apartments and the impressive Pissouri Beach hotel that has a large swimming pool and a good restaurant which caters for non-residents. There are also tavernas in the summer where you can enjoy Cypriot cooking. At the hotel, changing cabins and showers are available for a small charge.

The beach is long and provides good swimming except in some places where pebbles make it a little uncomfortable. Driving time about 45 minutes.

A longer journey further east will take you to AVDHIMOU Beach. This is very long and is an excellent beach where very few people go. A taverna provides all the basic facilities. The jetty was used in the past for the export of local produce. It is used by many British servicemen from the base nearby.

View of the Bay at Pissouri, developed recently as a small tourist resort.

MOUNTAIN EXCURSIONS

These trips will take you high up into the mountains, to the edge of the Troodos Mountain Range, where the forest is very interesting. The road up to Panayia is good and wide most of the way and passes through some old and famous vineyards. The aim of the trip is to visit Khrysorroyiatissa Monastery (26 miles from Paphos); or the famous Cedar Valley and Stavros tis Psokas. The return trip could be by the same route; or one could make the return journey by carrying on through Pentalia and Amargeti, although this route is very twisting and requires more care. However, the scenery is breathtaking. One could even take this route first and return the other way. Whatever one decides, this is a worthwhile journey.

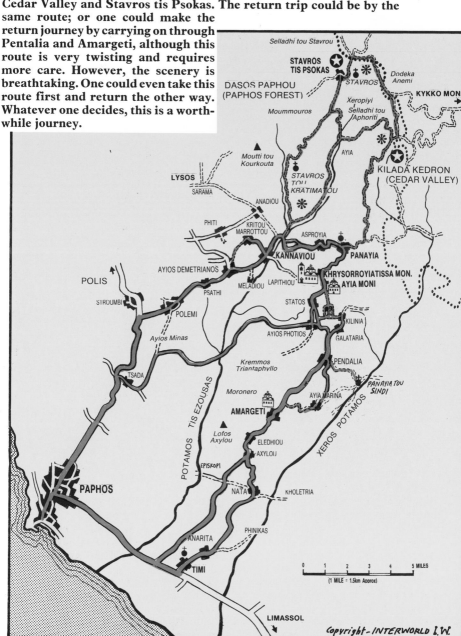

View of Panayia villages with its dominant church as seen from Khrysorroyiatissa monastery.

ROUTE B-1
TO PANAYIA and KHRYSORROYIATISSA MONASTERY via POLEMI

Here you proceed along the main road PAPHOS-POLIS. After climbing through the mountains, you pass Tsada and then you descend toward Stroumbi. Just before the village you turn right to **POLEMI.**

This, like all the surrounding villages, is vine growing country. Its fertile land also grows cereal and other products, thus it has become a main agricultural centre.

The road is good and wide. After Polemi you reach PSATHI, a small village and the countryside becomes more mountainous. The views of the valleys below and the Troodos mountains in the distance are very impressive.

AYIOS DHIMITRIANOS, built on the side of the mountain is a good place for views. From here, a road branches out west (see below B-2).

Descending down the valley, you reach a village, rich in greenery, **KANNAVIOU.**

In olden days when the roads were narrow and the trip up to here would have taken twice as long, it was a necessary stopping place. This is still a good idea. You can relax on your trips upwards to the mountains at one of the cafes under enormous trees, cool and refreshing.

Through the edges of the southern part of the Paphos Forest and climbing up steep roads you reach **PANAYIA.** The last village in this region, a small but proud village dominated by its church. It is famous as the village was the birthplace of Makarios, the great Religious and Political leader. He eventually became the first President of the Republic.

In the village you can visit the house where he was born. Personal belongings and other items are exhibited there.

The views from here are spectacular and for those with a few hours to kill it is an ideal place from which to explore the countryside.

Beyond here to the north is the forest of Paphos and tracks will take you to Stavros tis Psokas (see below).

From Panayia it is a short drive to the monastery.

The monastery of Khrysorroyiatissa with its living quarters, wine cellars and shops selling "homemade" wines and other products.

MAKARIOS, the world famous Cypriot Statesman, politician, and Archbishop of Cyprus, was born in Panayia village on August 13, 1913, the son of a shepherd. At an early age he left the goats and sheep and became a novice at Kykko Monastery. At the age of 37 he became Archbishop, religious and political leader. Since the 50's he symbolized everything that was Cyprus and actively participated in the struggles of Freedom. He became President of the newly formed Republic in 1960. He died on 3rd August 1977. A legend to live forever.

MONASTERY OF KHRYSORROYIATISSA

This is a delightful monastery, built on the side of Royia mountain, some 2768 feet high with a wonderful view of the surrounding valleys and villages. It was founded in 1152AD by a monk called Ignatius. He also discovered the miraculous icon of the Virgin Mary, which was painted by St. Luke The Evangelist. The legend says that the icon was thrown into the sea during the Iconoclastic Wars in Isauria and was washed up on the beach of Moulia, near Yeroskipos, along the coast of Paphos.

A fisherman kept it in a cave nearby where it was found four Centuries later by the monk Ignatius. The Franks, and then the Turks, persecuted the monastery and it was only in the 18th Century that it was allowed to function freely. It was at this time that most of the buildings were erected. Abbots were ordained from 1770AD. During the Greek mainland revolution of 1821 the monastery had shown some resistance against the Turks, and it was soon to be occupied by the Turkish army and suffered much damage.

Abbot Kyrillos Georgiades managed to revive it in later times. In 1967 a fire destroyed most of the monastery, but it was restored soon afterwards. Around the monastery there are plantations of apple trees, cherry trees etc.

Inside the picturesque church there are treasures and beautiful icons, the most famous being that of The Virgin Mary Khrysorroyiatissa (18th Century). The monastery has an interesting collection of Holy Gospels, books or religious music, manuscripts, religious ornaments and crosses. Overnight accommodation is available and during the summer you are advised to contact the monastery beforehand to secure a vacancy. There is also a restaurant and cafeteria, with spectacular views over the valley.

One of the monks most recent endeavours is Wine Making thus reviving old traditions. A small winery produces excellent wine which can be purchased here.

AYIA MONI

Ayia Moni is around 2kms south of the monastery of **Khrysorroyiatissa**. The church, one of the oldest in Cyprus being established in the 4th century AD was erected on the site of an ancient and important Temple, that of **Hera.** Some inscriptions were found among the foundations in the Cypriote Character and other places, in ancient Greek. The church is dedicated to *St. Nickolas.* The monastery buildings, some dating to 1638 and 1820 have been partially restored. They form a "U" shape and have a courtyard.

Ayia Moni is situated in a unique and very favourable spot, the right choice for a temple and a monastic retreat. The cliffs of *Aetokremmos* mountain surround it from 3 sides forming a half moon shape, thus averting every wind except from the west side. A spring, famous through the district for its purity, runs below providing water and greenery.

Profitis Elias, a small chapel high up the mountain of *Ayia* some 2 miles east of Khrysorroyiatissa mon. and north east of Ayia Moni is of no great interest except for its unique scenic views. It is situated on the highest spot and dedicated to Profitis Elias, the Saint of rain, thunder and lightning. You can reach this place on foot only, ideal for country walkers and explorers.

In times of long periods of drought, people used to gather at the monastery of Khrysorroyiatissa and process the icon of The Virgin to Ayia Moni (ruined chapel of Ayios Efthymios) and from there climb up the mountain to the chapel of Profitis Elias for prayers.

The place has been renovated recently, with living quarters and one plan is to make it a centre of icon preservation.

Left: Ayia Moni as now restored.
Right: Khrysorroyiatissa Monastery church entrance and bell tower.

Just one view of the ever changing scenery of Paphos Forest. Stavros tis Psokas Forestry station.

ROUTE B-2
TO THE FOREST OF PAPHOS

The Forest of Paphos, arguably the most beautiful in the Middle East, covers most of the north-eastern part of Paphos stretching into the Western Nicosia district. It is largely inaccessible.

The existing roads are narrow and generally unsurfaced so make sure that you have good transport. Only 4 wheel drive is suitable.

STAVROS TIS PSOKAS

After Kannaviou you take the road towards Stavros tis Psokas: this is an interesting valley in a beautiful forest. Situated 33 miles from Paphos, this is the main rest area of the forest where beds are available in log cabins for a minimal charge. If you wish to stay and explore this lovely forest, telephone the Forestry Department in Nicosia, telephone 40-2264, to reserve accommodation.

Please remember that although the distance is short in miles it is long in driving time, as the road up to the mountains is twisting and narrow.

Stavros tis Psokas provides excellent and panoramic views of the surrounding countryside. Picnic sites are well established with special areas allocated for barbeque and souvla next to running cool water. The cafe close to the forestry station provides basic meals and snacks.

CEDAR VALLEY

You may reach this unique area of the Cyprus forest after visiting Stavros tis Psokas; or just before arriving at the village of Panayia, you take the mountain road towards the valley. The main characteristic of the forest is that most of the trees are CEDARS. From the area of Stavros to the Valley of Cedars you may be lucky enough to catch a glimpse of the national animal of Cyprus — **the Mouflon** — a wild but friendly animal belonging to the sheep family. This shy yet elegant animal is usually to be spotted in the early morning or late afternoon.

From the Cedar Valley you can reach the Kykko Monastery situated in the most idyllic part of the forest. The monastery is in the Nicosia district.

90

Above: A family gathering for "SOUVLA" at Stavros tis Psokas forest station. Facilities are available.
Below: One of the roads leading to Stavros tis Psokas.

In 1907 the late Sir Winston Churchill, as Under Secretary of State for the Colonies, visited Cyprus and was appalled by the state of the forest. He requested extra funds, of which most went to Stavros tis Psokas which was already, established as a forest station (1884). Now it is the headquarters of the forestry department controlling some ⅔rds of all Cyprus' Forests which we all enjoy and which plays such a great part in the island's economy.

This impressive stamp of the definitive issue of 1962 shows the Mouflon the animal loved not only in Paphos but in the whole of Cyprus. *(Courtesy, Cyprus Philatelic Bureaux).*

91

ROUTE B-3
TSADA—AYIOS PHOTIOS

From the Paphos-Polis road you turn into **TSADA** village. From here the views, below of Paphos town and the coastline are fascinating.

From here, a short but narrow road will take you to **STAVROS TIS MYTHRAS.** This small monastery can be reached from **Tsada** which is about 2½kms away. It is situated south east of the village and is part of a large property which is administered by the See of Paphos and served at one time as the official residence of the Bishop. The buildings provide some guest rooms and some of the doorways distinctly show a unique Gothic style. The present church is dated 1740. A text in ancient Cypriot writing was found here. In the monastery there is a large cross which was covered once with silver. Around 1834 there was a fierce fire in the monastery and an abbot seized the cross and threw it into the flames. The silver melted and extinguished the fire and some signs of the burning can

be seen on the cross. The surrounding area is full of vineyards.

From Tsada to Ayios Photios the road has been widened and is very pleasant crossing the **Valley of the Ezousas** River is exciting as it is very beautiful. The villages from Tsada onwards are **LETIMBOU,** with an interesting church; KOURTALA on the northern side of the road; LEMONA on the south and the large village of **KHOULOU.**

These villages are not of great importance as such but they are important for the vineyards which surround them.

Reaching Ayios Photios junction, you may go north towards Khrysorroyiatissa Monastery and the return journey, or turn right to the south to go back to Paphos through Amargeti and Timi.

Stavros tis Mythras monastery and surrounding vineyards *(Photo: Stephanos Theodorou)*

The old church of Amargeti.

ROUTE B-4
PAPHOS-PANAYIA
via TIMI

You take the road to Limassol and before the turning towards the airport, you turn left into **TIMI** village. Due to the fact that the airport is to the south and also because of its agricultural produce this area has become important. However signs have been found of an early bronze age civilization, also of Greek and Roman settlements. Timi is also known for its delicious **Louka-nika** (pork sausages) and **Halloumi** (goats cheese).

ANARITA is the next village and enjoys the honour of originating **Halloumi** cheese (the famous Cypriot goat cheese). **Anari** is the condensed whey which is produced as a by-product when making the cheese. Every May the *Halloumi Festival* is held here. To the south of the village are the remains of the Byzantine monastery of *Ayios Onesiforos*.

A new, by-pass road, before Timi will take you directly to Axylou thus saving a bit of time on the journey. This route gives you panoramic views.

The road then starts to climb upwards and is narrow in places. Care must be taken around the bends.

NATA—AXYLOU—ELEDHIOU are the next villages, mainly agricultural, with vineyards, almond trees, carobs, olives, citrus trees and cattle.

AMARGETI: This is a large village, the main centre of the region and has a large square with numerous kafenia. The domed church also has an interesting tower. It is a village with an ancient history which includes not only medieval settlements but remains of a life which existed as far back as the Bronze age. There are some ruins of a Temple dedicated to **Apollo Menthius** (the healer of the sick) which dates back to c.400BC.

A large number of small votive objects including doves, statuettes, phallic objects, cones, bunches of grapes etc. were found in the area and also inscriptions with strange dedications; all were discovered by D.H. Hogarth in 1887-88.

The ruins are outside the village and to explore them, you must ask the villagers to point out the place, although many may not be aware of the actual location.

PENDALIA: An interesting church with an old icon. Ancient tombs were found by the side of the chalky cliff overlooking the village and also to the south.

93

Above: General view of Pendalia with its church. *Below:* The newly built church of Statos Village which has moved from its old site. The church contains some modern, well executed wall paintings and frescoes.

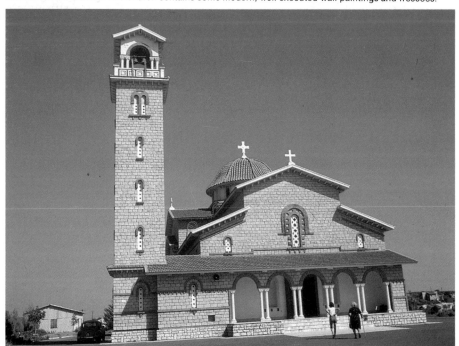

Panayia tou Sindi in the Spring, visited mainly by local shepherds. *(Photo: David Pearlman (Exalt Travel Ltd).)*

AYIOS PHOTIOS junction is a small settlement and the old village has been abandoned; then you reach **STATOS** situated on a plateau. It is famous for its Cypriot food specialities known to lovers of mezé as **Loukanika** (spicy sausages) and **Lountza** (smoked pork meat). The village has been enlarged with tree lined roads and a newly built church which has been decorated with modern frescoes in the old Byzantine style and well worth viewing. It is the birthplace of the new Archbishop of Cyprus, Chrysostomos.

In the surrounding area some monolithic stones have been observed by travellers in the past together with traces of old habitations.

Further on is Moni and the monastery of Khrysorroyiatissa and then Panayia.

PANAYIA TOU SINDI

This isolated church in the heart of the river Xeros Potamos valley is off the main track and unknown not only to most visitors to Paphos but also to locals. It can be reached most easily from the villages of Pendalia or Ayia Marina (see main route) or from the east from Salamiou (see next section route). Even better, you can join the specialist exploration excursions run by EXALT. The church's structure still survives and dominates the valley but other buildings are in ruins with only a few walls standing. What makes the church so interesting is its isolated position and the impressive scenery.

A view of Dhrinia village and the surrounding area.

ROUTE B-5
TO PHITI

Returning back to Ayios Demetrianos, if you have time during the same day or on a return trip, you can explore another side of Paphos' countryside.

From **Ayios Demitrianos** (see route B-1) you turn to the west and after a short drive a left turning will take you to **DHRINIA**, a small village, but if you continue you pass south of **MILIA** and reach **LASA**, another village with a modern church. All these 3 villages and the surrounding countryside, are picturesque, and best seen during spring.

From Lasa, turn right and you reach **PHITI** with old, usually empty houses and narrow streets. It is famed for its embroidery, unique to the Paphos area. Local women weave and embroider beautiful items which are worth purchasing. Please consult someone at the cafe in the square. Phiti is also famous for its **"moonshine"** — an alcoholic spirit called **Zivania** which is over 90% strong (pure spirit) and is exported to Russia for making Vodka; it is made from the remains of grapes that have

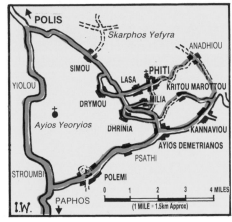

been already used for making wine. The church in the main square is again of some interest.

For your return journey you can proceed westward to **DHRYMOU** whose church is interesting. Some ancient ruins were discovered here, believed to be of a **Temple of Apollo Hylates** but apart from some megalithic stones there isn't much to be seen.

Further west is **SIMOU** a very nice agricultural village. From here you may

Above: The church and square of Phiti village. The monument to the left is erected by the villagers to those who emigrated to foreign lands but did not forget their origin and with funds helped the village by bringing water. *Below right:* The famous Phitiotika lace.

attempt to visit the gorge of *Potamos tou Stavrou tis Psokas* and the old bridge of *Skarphos* and explore the remote countryside. However, the road is very rough.

Back at Simou, you continue your journey through absorbing countryside and you reach the main road Paphos-Polis. If you have time to spare, you turn right towards Polis or turn left for Paphos, only a 20 minute drive.

The roads in general are wide, in good condition and are covered with asphalt.

TA PHITIOTIKA

These beautiful embroideries and woven artifacts can match those from Lefkara. However as Phiti and Paphos are more isolated they have not acquired the same fame. The patterns and designs, originating in Phiti, are copied by other Paphos villages.

Items can be purchased from many shops in Paphos town.

EXPLORE THE VALLEY OF DHIARIZOS

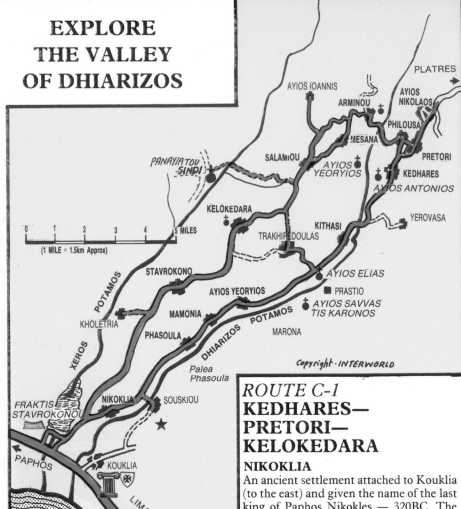

This is an area worth exploring and it will take more or less a day to complete. Refreshments can be bought from the Kafenion in any of the villages along the route, although a meal may not be that easy to find. A packed lunch would do nicely.

Along the main Paphos—Limassol road you turn left before Kouklia, towards the newly built Asprokremmos Dam (Stavrokonos) — the largest in Cyprus which you can observe from the top. At the road junction you follow the sign for Nikoklia (should you decide to take the left turning, you go up the route the other way round).

ROUTE C-1
KEDHARES— PRETORI— KELOKEDARA

NIKOKLIA

An ancient settlement attached to Kouklia (to the east) and given the name of the last king of Paphos Nikokles — 320BC. The modern village is scenic and situated by the west bank of the river. The old church has several interesting icons.

Recently it has been developed as a village with some British residents settling here.

SOUSKIOU-VATHYRKAKAS

Situated between Kouklia 2km to the northeast and Souskiou village 1.5km to the southwest. An important Chalcolithic settlement. Finds include pendants, female figurines and the largest statuette of that period found in Cyprus, illegally exported and now in private hands in Europe. The area is fenced. Tombs of other periods were discovered close by.

Above: Fraktis (Dam) of Stavrokonou *(Courtesy Joannou & Paraskevaides).*
Below: One of the scenic routes along the Dhiarizos Valley.

SOUSKIOU

Of no great importance, but an ancient neolithic settlement was found by the side of the banks of the river with tombs and artifacts etc.

MAMONIA a small agricultural village amongst orange groves.

AYIOS YEORYIOS — small village. On the north east, by the west side of the river is an old rock cut tomb with the chapel of *Ayios Elias* built by its side. Over the other side of the river is the abandoned settlement of **Prastio** and a late 15th century chapel, now deserted.

Just around a km south west of Prastio are the remains of a once prosperous monastery, **Ayios Savvas tis Karonos.** This isolated monastery is of unknown origin but it is believed it was established in the 12th-13th century. An inscription written in 1501 on the west door reads:

"It must be that a king first built this monastery, which time has so damaged. May God on the awful day of Judgement remember the Evarch of this monastery who in 1501 repaired and beautified this church".

The existing church has some interesting icons and is in good condition. Both the church and some buildings show gothic influence and have good carved stone work.

In 1568 a fire destroyed the monastery. According to Abbot Gerasimus who sent a letter to king James II, it was struck by lightning and all the monastery, except the church, was destroyed. The king agreed to have it rebuilt on condition that a mass was said forever for his soul.

Some of the buildings are now used by farmers. The only way to reach this place is by foot.

After **KITHASI** the road starts climbing upwards and the view of the river and the valley is really beautiful. To the left is the restored church of *Ayios Antonios.*

KEDHARES. A picturesque small village and the agricultural centre of the region. From here the views below of the Dhiarizos valley are excellent.

PRETORI — The church has an interesting 16th century icon of the Virgin. It is believed that the name Pretori was given from a Roman general called Prator who had a summer villa here.

From here, if you follow the road that twists up north, you go to Platres through the village of AYIOS NICOLAOS. Up to 1928 the 13th century church in the village had two altars, one Latin and one Orthodox. From Ayios Nicolaos, if you have lots of time to spare, you can continue your

Left: The chapel of Ayios Elias as seen from the main road. *Right:* An old house of Kedhares village.

General view of a geologically interesting countryside near the village of Kedhares.

journey upwards over twisting mountain roads to reach the resort of **PLATRES.** Turning towards the west and down the valley through **PHILOUSA** and then up the other side you reach **ARMINOU.** Armenian refugees used to live here. The church of *Stavros* is of 18th century.

AYIOS IOANNIS situated to the north of the main road. This was a Turkish village but the inhabitants went to the north of Cyprus and most of the houses are now empty. To the north is the truck road leading to the Bridge of Roudhias.

MESANA — A small village with vineyards. Down in the river valley by the south east of the village is the isolated church of *Ayios Yeoryios* where there used to be a monastery. There are some interesting icons.

SALAMIOU — A big village with a large impressive church. The village, like all the others of the area, produces some grapes but mainly almonds, carobs and sheep.

KELOGEDARA

An interesting village with scenic views of the valley to the west of the river Xeros Potamos where the remains of the 14th-15th century monastery of *Santi* can be seen (see previous section route B-5). The CHURCH OF *Panayia Elousa* is famous for its hexagonal dome.

After driving through the village of *STAVROGONNOU* you eventually reach the junction from where you went to Nikoklia, back to the main road to Paphos.

At present an American-Canadian team of archaeologists headed by Prof. David Rupp of Ontario University is carrying out a systematic archaeological survey for the department of antiquities. Some of their discoveries are very interesting in relation to past history of the area.

Panoramic view of Xeros Potamos Valley as taken from the main road at the junction to Galataria.

ROUTE C-2
TO PERAVASA—
VRETSIA

To reach this isolated area you can either join the EXALT excursions or use a strong car. This journey must not be attempted with an ordinary car. The track roads were old camel routes.

Peravasa from Arminou. The area is virgin and ideal for well equipped explorers who will be rewarded with its beauty.

PERVASA is an abandoned old settlement. Further west is the narrow gorge of the **EZOUSAS RIVER** and the **ROUDHIAS BRIDGE,** of Venetian origin. Here in the locality, according to the British explorer D.G. Hogarth — 1888; "There is a mill and in the ground and near the mill a sculptured stele representing 2 female and a male figures. The clumsy lines of the drapery recall the statuettes found in Amargeti. The interest of the stele is that there are no known ancient sites in the area. Who then brought this heavy stele here and why?"

The hamlets of **VRETSIA** is the next stop, used mainly by farmers and shepherds.

Back in civilization is the small village of KILINIA and then the larger village of

GALATARIA which has an interesting church. From here you get into the road to Paphos or Panayia.

Galataria Village.

102

ROUTE D-1
TO EPISKOPI

This is a short but very interesting scenic journey for an afternoon or morning outing. Go through the north east part of Paphos town and pass the Youth Hostel (Eleftherios Venizelos Avenue). After a short drive, on the left there is a road going to **ANAVARGOS** and then to the right is **KONIA,** a very popular place for British people to settle. They enjoy panoramic views of the coastline.

Further up there is a crossroad. To the left is **ARMOU** where there are some tombs, remains of a Roman villa and panoramic views of Paphos. To the right is **MARATHOUNDHA,** where there are ruined churches in the countryside. The church of

"Aetokremmos" — The huge rock-mountain on the entrance to Episkopi village.

Above: Episkopi and Ezousas river and valley. No doubt, this place is a paradise with lovely scenery.
Left: One view of the main road leading to Episkopi area. The blue boxes on the right are for the bees, producing honey.

the village is interesting and there is a limestone altar with large letters in script of the Ptolemaic period. *"Apolloni Myrati Xanthos Ipper Onasa Viskon"*. Signs of a Temple were found believed to be that of Apollo.

EPISKOPI

About 10 miles from Paphos. Situated in the fertile valley of the *Ezousas river* and has beautiful views. Late Roman remains were found here. This, together with other examples of Roman settlements, prove that not only Nea Paphos and the coastal area were inhabited by Romans and earlier peoples, but that they spread all over the countryside.

There is a 12-13th century church which is of some interest, dedicated to *Ayios Hilarion* who came here from Palestine where he introduced monastic life, and spent his last years in a cave which is outside the village. According to St. Jerome

". . . he entered Paphos, that city of Cyprus so nobly celebrated by the poets, which destroyed by frequent earthquakes, has now only its ruins to show that once it was . . ."

When St. Hilarion died in Episkopi he was buried here but his followers stole the corpse and took it back to Palestine.

104

TO AYIOS NEOPHYTOS MONASTERY

ROUTE E-1
AYIOS NEOPHYTOS—TALA—EMBA

This is a short trip to the famous monastery of Ayios Neophytos. To reach the monastery, one turns left at Mesoyi village and follows the road through the neighbouring small village of Trimithousa, which was once an estate given in 1375 AD to Sir Theobald Belfarage by King Peter II, for his services against the Genoese invaders.

View of Ayios Neophytos monastery from the Enclistra.

AYIOS NEOPHYTOS MONASTERY

This is an impressive collection of buildings, with a courtyard and church in the centre. Adjoining the monastery there is a restaurant built into the side of the hill, just above the village of Tala. Taking the climb to the top of the hill one is able to enjoy the fantastic view over the valley below, looking towards the villages of Emba, Kissonerga and even as far as the Coral Bay area. The view takes in all the surrounding district, right down to the coast.

The monastery was founded by Ayios Neophytos, one of the most important Saints in Cyprus. He arrived in Paphos around 1159AD. He cut three caves from the rock at the side of the hill, far above the ground, giving him shelter and security and he stayed there as a hermit. Steps lead up to the cave, which is called Enclistra. There are many frescoes, some painted under the supervision of the Saint himself, they are in very good condition and are to be admired. Other frescoes in the cave were painted around the 15th Century. These are:

In The Nave
Abraham and Three Angels (south wall)
A Group of Various Saints (west wall)

105

Subjects from The New Testament (upper wall)
St. Helena and Constantine The Great (east wall)

In The Bema
Various Saints — Ephraim, Hilarion, Theodoros (north and west walls)
The Prayer of Prophesis (east wall)
Christ The Pantokrator (roof)
The Ascension (ceiling)
St. Neophytos between The Archangels Gabriel and Michael, who lead him to Christ on the Day of Judgement.

In The Cell
Further frescoes can be seen here. This is the place where the Saint used to sleep and measures only 8 feet by 11 feet. The Saint also had a library and stone table in this room.

The main buildings around the church, some of them built more recently, are used by the monks as living quarters. There is also some space where visitors can stay overnight.

The Church
This building, interesting from the outside, is even better inside, with frescoes and paintings in pure Byzantine style. They are

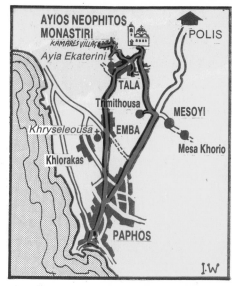

all stated to be 15th Century.
The icons which cover the iconostasi are also worth seeing, as are the carved wooden statues.
The Church is dedicated to The Virgin Mary, although the name of Ayios Neophytos is given to the church by many people.
Apart from the superb wall paintings of the Enclistra the visitor can enjoy interesting wall paintings inside the Church. Also to be seen are woodcarvings. The sacred skull of the Saint is kept inside a silver case and has a pyramid-shaped cover. The wooden-carved Iconostasi displays very artistic Icons. More treasures can be seen in the small museum of the monastery.
The whole area around the monastery has enormous beauty and is surrounded by vineyards, trees, gardens and running water. It is a very popular place and visited by many people, so if you would prefer to visit at a quiet time, a visit at the beginning of the week rather than weekends is recommended.

Biography of The Saint
Ayios Neophytos was born near Lefkara in the village of Kato-Dris (Limassol — Larnaca area) in 1134AD. When he was 18 he entered the monastery of Ayios Chrysostomos and here he learned to read and write. He visited the Holy Places in Jerusalem, but on his return to Cyprus he

AYIOS NEOPHYTOS — Icon of St. Mark dating to the 15th cent.

106

The ENCLISTRA where Ayios Neophytos used to live and preach. The wall paintings are in the lower part.

Wall painting of Christ the Pantocrator (the Creator of All) from the Enclistra wall paintings.

Fresco of the Three Saints which is in the church.

decided to find a place that was quiet to rest his life and soul in isolation. He at last arrived at this place which he created as his monastery. Whilst in isolation he wrote many hymns and books dedicated to The Virgin Mary, Holy Cross and Jesus Christ. He also wrote the Fifty Chapter Bible. Also famous is the letter in which he describes the occupation of Cyprus by Richard Coeur de Lion, entitled "Concerning the Misfortunes of Cyprus". During the latter years of his life he became famous and many people came to listen to his teachings. Many people who came wanted to help and become monks.

In 1170AD his work was honoured by the Bishop of Paphos, Basil Kinnamos, who ordained him as a priest. He died around 1219, at the age of 85 (or thereabouts).

Many of his manuscripts survive today and in the monastery there is a workshop which is restoring all that is left and binding it into books.

The discovery of Ayios Neophytos Tomb.

When Cyprus was occupied by the Turks in 1571, the monks of the monastery sealed off the Enclistra and the saints tomb and painted a frescoe to conceal the door and its surroundings where it can be seen now. It was re-discovered some 200 years later in 1757 as follows: A monk of the monastery, believing that there was treasure inside the Enclistra, discovered the sealed door and one night broke it open and to his surprise found a tomb. While he was attempting to remove the stone covering it he was suddenly struck down by a mysterious force. When he recovered his senses, he rushed to see the abbot and told him of his discovery. Early in the morning the abbot and the monks went to the Enclistra and saw the tomb and inside the grave found the body of Ayios Neophytos clad in the garments which he had himself woven and girt with the iron girdle which he had worn during his lifetime.

Right: The holy door of the church by the iconostasi.
Below: Entrance with wall paintings at the Enclistra.

The living quarters of the monastery.

THE RETURN TRIP

Leaving the monastery you may return to Paphos via Tala and Emba. The road goes through the hills where a modern village is growing with new villas that have beautiful views of the coastline. It is popular with British families who have settled here.

Between Tala and the Monastery and in the surrounding Hills to the east and west, a new town has emerged over the last few years.

Many developers have contributed to this but most credit must be given to the enterprising Mr Leptos. The **KAMARES** village is a tourist complex of detached houses and other apartments with a square, swimming pool, art centre and leisure facilities.

No Paphian ever believed that someone would succeed in establishing anything in such bare and hostile land. They were proved wrong. The views are breathtaking.

Swimming pool commanding panoramic views at Kamares village.

TALA is in contrast to the modern village. You go through the narrow main roads with its old houses. To the west of the square is the church of *Ayia Ekaterini*. About 3 miles to the northwest of the village an early Cypriot cemetery was found recently.

EMBA is a large village with about 1000 inhabitants. Spring is an ideal time to enjoy the countryside around the village when the fields are full of wild flowers and cyclamen. The word *Emba* means *Entrance* and it was, in fact, the western entrance to Paphos. It was an important place during the Frankish period and was one of the 5 Bailiwicks into which the Paphos district was divided.

The church of the *Virgin Mary Khryseleousa* is of great importance and dates to the 13th century with later additions. There are beautiful icons and the frescoe of the New Testament, but unfortunately, most of the other frescoes have been very crudely restored.

To the south of the village is the small chapel of *Ayios Limpros* and a cave called *Petridia* which is natural and has stalactites. The water is believed to cure a variety of skin diseases.

EMBA-Wall painting in the church of Panayia Mary Khryseleousa representing the miracle of fishing 15th cent. AD.

Above: Kamares village near Ayios Neophytos. In the far distance is Coral Bay.
Below: Emba village church of Panayia Khryseleousa is of Byzantine architecture.

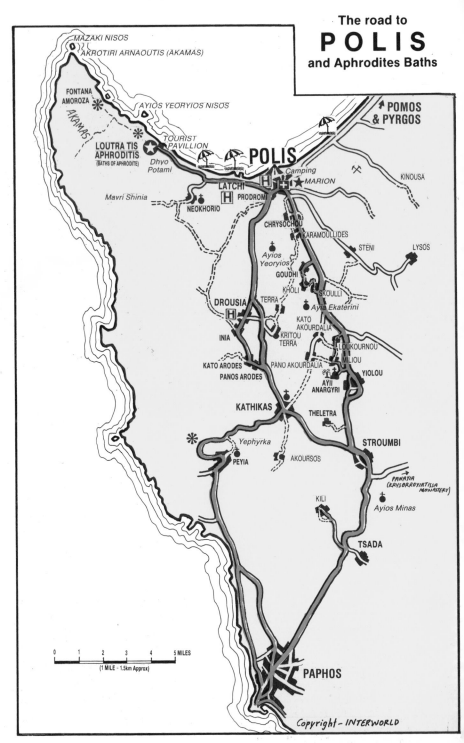

The road to
POLIS
and Aphrodites Baths

MAZAKI NISOS
AKROTIRI ARNAOUTIS (AKAMAS)

FONTANA
AMOROZA

AKAMAS

AYIOS YEORYIOS NISOS

TOURIST
PAVILLION

LOUTRA TIS
APHRODITIS
(BATHS OF APHRODITE)

Dhyo
Potami

Mavri Shinia

POLIS

Camping

★ MARION

POMOS
& PYRGOS

KINOUSA

LATCHI
PRODROMI
NEOKHORIO

CHRYSOCHOU

KARAMOULLIDES

STENI

LYSOS

Ayios
Yeoryios

GOUDHI

KHOLI

SKOULLI

Ayia Ekaterini

DROUSIA

TERRA

INIA

KRITOU
TERRA

KATO
AKOURDALIA

LOUKOURNOU

MILIOU

KATO ARODES

PANOS ARODES

PANO AKOURDALIA

AYII
ANARGYRI

YIOLOU

KATHIKAS

THELETRA

Yephyrka

PEYIA

AKOURSOS

STROUMBI

PANAYIA
(KRYSORROYIATISSA
MONASTERY)

KILI

Ayios Minas

TSADA

0   1   2   3   4   5 MILES
(1 MILE = 1.5km Approx)

PAPHOS

Copyright - INTERWORLD

112

PAPHOS TO POLIS

There are two routes to Polis and the Baths of Aphrodite and you may go one way and return the other, thus making the trip more interesting as the roads are very good. In fact, there is a third route going along the coastal road towards Coral Bay, then turning to Peyia and from there via Arodhes.

ROUTE F-1
Via YIOLOU

To the left of the junction to **TSADA** (see route B-3) you go towards **KILI,** a small village commanding a panoramic view of the coastline. There is the chapel of *Ayios Mamas* above the village and to the south is *Ayia Varvara* chapel. Other chapels are in ruins. There are also caves *(Kyra Vrisi)* but take care if you risk entering them.

Pass Tsada and you reach **STROUMBI,** population about 700. This a famous centre for vineyards producing excellent wine and mentioned by Lawrence Durrell in his book about life in Cyprus *"Bitter Lemons".* A Frankish Estate was established here.

THELEDRA is to the left of the main road, on the side of a hill. The church dated 1755 has interesting icons. Local women produce good embroidery but in the past it was known as the ideal place for shepherds to bring their sheep during the summer months due to the abundant vegetation, thus the name was given *"Golden Theledra".* Around the area are traces of Neolithic settlements and ruins of a medieval church.

YIOLOU — Another wine centre. Its 19th century church is of interest. The surrounding area and the hills up to Theledra are wonderful during the spring, full of beautiful flowers called Matsikorida.

AYII ANARGYRI. An old monastic complex, built around 1649 believed to be on the site of a stone age settlement. It was founded by the brothers Cosmas and Damianos, a generous duo who gave their services to the poor. Now it is a centre for Mineral Baths due to its famous therapeutic waters. The sulphur baths are helpful to many ailments, including rheumatism, arthritis, spinal problems, gastritis ulcers etc. There is also a small hotel.

A short diversion will take you from here west towards **MILIOU** where traces of old

A general view of Ayii Anargyri *(Courtesy Ayii Anargyri hotel).*

habitation were found, then north to Pano and Kato **AKOURDALIA** with interesting scenery and a nice church, then back to the main road.

LOUKOURNOU, SKOULLI, KHOLI are to the left of the main road by the side of hills. Citrus trees are to be seen in the narrow gorges. **KHOLI** has a beautiful church, that of *Arkhangelos Michael,* dating to the 13th century with icons and wall paintings of the 16th century. According to tradition, the church was part of the former monastery of **Archangel Michael** which is now in ruins.

• REPTILES OF CYPRUS •
At Skoulli village, by the main road, there's a permanent small exhibition of live Amphibia and Reptiles which is organised by the Herpetological Society of Cyprus.

GOUDHI — A citrus centre to the left. Ancient tombs were found here.

CHRYSOCHOU — Comes from the Greek word meaning gold and it is believed that some gold mines were operating here in the past. The land is very fertile and under the Turks it served as a centre of local administration.

ROUTE F-2
Via KATHIKAS

After **STROUMBI** turn left and you reach **KATHIKAS**. Apart from its wine, it is famous for producing excellent **Sultanas, Sutzoukos** (a product of grape juice, sugar, flour, almonds — a kind of quince paste); **Palouze** (a product of grape juice, sugar, flour — a kind of blancmange sweet). Also **Trahanas** (an ingredient for soup — a product of wheat dried in the sun in cubes). Ancient tombs were discovered here.

ARODES (Pano = Upper — Kato = Lower). The name Arodes originated from the island of Rhodes and was the property of the Knights of St. John of Jerusalem (Hospitallers). Around the countryside even up to Peyia and Kathikas are traces of Tombs and according to the explorer Hogarth who visited the area in 1887-88,

"sarcophaghi, pottery and glass of Roman origin were found". He also mentioned *"near Pano Orodhes (Arodhes) a mile and a half down the slope and two miles above Lipati site is a unique specimen of a pierced monolith of unknown origin and near the stone are remains of a building".*

Left: The picturesque village of Goudhias seen from the main road. *Right:* Kathikas village with its narrow streets. *(Photo: Stephanos Theodorou).*

114

A typical "Mandra" — goats stable — a characteristic of Paphos rural areas and can be found in all the villages of the area.

INIA — small village, population 600.

DHROUSIA was originally settled by the Greek Arcadians. Recently a hotel Apartment was built here with panoramic views of the Polis bay. It was the result of a co-operative effort by the older villagers who emigrated to foreign lands. For lovers of the countryside it is an ideal spot to stay for a few days or longer.

A turning to the right takes you to **KRITOU TERRA** and to the nearby sister village of TERRA. Here are strong traces of Roman settlements. It was the birthplace of the famous *Haji Georghakis Kornesios* who was the great Dragoman (interpreter) of Cyprus from 1779-1809 and who gained great influence with the Turkish authorities. With his wealth he helped the poor and sick. Just over a mile to the northeast is the church of *Ayia Ekaterini* which can only be reached on foot. The large medieval church may be interesting to enthusiasts. It has three aisles and some frescoes but check in the village for the key.

Further down the road to Polis you pass, on the right, the shrine of *Ayios Yeoryios* built in the mouth of a cave probably in Byzantine times. At **PRODHROMI** a left turning will take you to **LATCHI** and **BATHS OF APHRODITE,** a right turning to POLIS.

POLIS

Silver coin of Marion — King Timochares (obverse) —5th Cent. B.C. *(Courtesy Director of Antiquities).*

Polis or **Polis tis Chrysochou** is an expanding agricultural and tourist centre with over 1700 inhabitants. There is a good hotel and self catering establishments. Between the town and the sea (about a mile away) is a well organised camping site — *see under accommodation.*

It can be used as a centre for excursions either to Akamas or the areas of Pomos and Pyrgos or the inland countryside and mountains. Some of the old buildings of Polis are very interesting and efforts have been made to restore some of them. Most of the main Banks have branches here and there is also a fruit and vegetable market. The two small churches are of some interest but the new church, although modern, is large and predominantly Byzantine in style. During the middle ages Polis was an important agricultural centre and the Turkish landowners used to breed stallions. It was here that the famous Paphos pony was bred.

Bichrome crater from Goudhi, 6th Cent. B.C. *(Courtesy Director of Antiquities, Cyprus Museum)*

> **Polis is now expanding as a small picturesque town attracting many visitors. Most come from Paphos on a day visit, but many prefer to stay here or the nearby Latchi area for a few days or for the whole of their holiday, where they enjoy the peace and quiet.**

Close to Polis to the east, was the ancient city of **MARION.** It was founded around the 10th century BC by Athenian settlers and for a short time flourished and influenced the surrounding areas. During the wars for the possession of the island between the Ptolemy of Egypt and Antigonus of Syria and Asia Minor, the king of Egypt, Ptolemy Lagus, attacked the city which came under the influence of Antigonus and it was razed to the ground in 312BC. Later in 285-247BC. Ptolemy Philadelphus rebuilt the city and renamed it **ARSINOE,** but it never regained its power and influence.

During the Frankish period it was renamed **POLIS** and here the Orthodox Bishop of Paphos was exiled in 1222AD.

There is nothing to be seen of the old Kingdom, all the buildings were destroyed and it was stated that seamen bringing timber to this area from Cilicia in Asia

Right: Attic lekythos — 6th Cent. B.C. *Left:* Funerary relief stele of Onasis — 5th Cent. B.C. Both from Marion. *(Courtesy Director of Antiquities).*
Below: The modern church of Apostolos Andreas.

116

Above and below: Two scenes from Polis town.

Minor, returned with stones of the ruined buildings. Around 1886 some 441 tombs were found. Further excavations were carried out in 1889, 1891 and 1929, most of the finds were taken abroad and those that remained in the island are exhibited at the museum of Paphos and the Cyprus Museum — Nicosia. The tombs were afterwards covered.

As we go to press we noticed that Polis has embarked on a very well planned restoration project which includes old buildings, squares and other amenities.

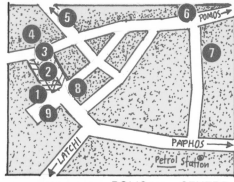

POLIS town CENTRE
(not on scale)

(1) Ayios Nicolaos Church
(2) Square with Cafes and Shops
(3) Ayia Kyriaki Church
(4) Hospital
(5) Road to Camping and to Beach
(6) Apostolos Andreas Church
(7) Site of Ancient Marion
(8) Fruit & Vegetable Market
(9) Parking

Above: The camping area of Polis, a well organised site next to the beach.
Below: The long Polis beach which, most of the time, is only for the few.

118

ROUTE F-3
PAPHOS—POLIS—
BATHS OF APHRODITE

LATCHI

Taking the road east of Polis and passing close to the beach and sea, one reaches a very picturesque fishing harbour, **LAT-CHI.** The place is well-known for its fresh fish which one can eat in the tavernas around the protected harbour. The view of the small fishing boats is delightful. Overnight accommodation can be found here, or at Polis. There are sandy beaches close by for swimming, and the surrounding countryside with the low hills is worth exploring. The area around the small harbour is now expanding with some hotels and self-catering apartments, better beach facilities and numerous tavernas.

The Latchi fishing harbour has just been widened, dredged and landscaped with paved areas round the edges for easy access to boats and pedestrian walkways.

It is slowly becoming one of the most important attractions of the Paphos district.

Right left and below: Two scenes from the picturesque Latchi harbour with its colourful boats.

BATHS OF APHRODITE

Driving further away from Polis, close to the sea, the road twists and turns and comes to an end at The **Baths of Aphrodite**. Here there is a small tourist pavilion which serves food — including good fish — and drinks. Below there is a small beach, mainly pebbles, but the water is crystal clear. The sea is ideal for underwater exploration and diving clubs often visit the area. Above, (among the carob trees), you may camp freely.

The main purpose of our trip is to visit the Baths of Aphrodite which are within

Below: The water drops winter and summer, continuously in this pool, where Aphrodite used to come with her lover.

LOCATION OF APHRODITES BATHS

(1) **TOURIST PAVILION/ RESTAURANT**
(2) **PEBBLED BEACH**
(3) **CAR PARK**
(4) **BATHS OF APHRODITE**
(5) **TRUCK ROAD** leading to Fontana Amoroza (5 miles)

(6) **FOREST** (camping allowed)
(7) **ROCK** offshore
(8) **Excellent views of the Coastline**
(9) **Island**

Map Not in Scale

120

The coast around the Baths of Aphrodite with crystal clear waters.

Above and *Below:* Two more views of the beautiful coastal area around the Baths of Aphrodite, better seen in late Spring and early Autumn.

walking distance from the tourist pavilion. The bathing place of Aphrodite is a semi-cave draped with cool vegetation. Water drips down from a spring at the top into a pool of water. If one bathes in the pool, eternal youth would be bestowed, but unfortunately it is not permitted to enter the water. The legend says that Aphrodite used to bathe here at the cave because of the coolness of the spring water after her wanderings in the forest. The legend also says that Aphrodite used to bring her young lovers here, away from the eyes of the people. The thick vegetation around the spring makes the place idyllic.

Five miles further west, near the far end of the peninsula, is the Spring of Love — FONTANA AMOROSA as the poets called it. The area is uninhabited, but of great beauty, with one side being high mountains and the other rocky or sandy bays. If you are lucky enough to find the spot, you will see that there is nothing of importance to mark the place, but it is nevertheless well worth a visit.

You will get a feeling of enormous joy just being in surroundings which inspired poets so much. The best way is to walk, since the road is not suitable for cars. It's about 5-6 miles walk. Alternatively, ask a fisherman at Latchi. For a small fee he may take you there.

In the area around the Baths of Aphrodite and near the sea, artifacts of a chalcolithic period were recently discovered. Previous travellers and explorers mentioned that near the spring, old ruins were found, believed to be those of the lost colony of the Athenian settlement of Akamandes. Along the coastline in the sea bed, a mass of Roman pottery was found.

Ayios Yeoryios Island
There is an interesting tradition regarding the Byzantine hero Dhighenis. While here with his love, the Queen Regena *(see Petra tou Dhigeni - Paphos)* they had a quarrel. Queen Regena left him and tried to get away in a boat. In his rage he took a great rock which he threw at the boat; the rock missed and split into 3 pieces, the largest formed an island that is Ayios Yeoryios.

Below: This area is for those who venture away from the swimming pool. (Those who know how to enjoy the real nature of Paphos).

Three views of
the Fontana
Amoroza area
which can be
reached either by
boat or by a long
walk from the
Baths area. To do
this you require
good shoes and
lots of water.

Above: A ship
wreck.
Left: Remains of
old mines.
Below: Coastal
scenery.

ROUTE FG-1
POLIS TO PYRGOS

Although Pyrgos is under the Nicosia area, it is administered also from Paphos at present, because, since the Turkish occupation of the Lefka area, the coastal road has been cut off and it is difficult to connect with Nicosia. The trip from Polis is long but exciting. However, you can drive as far as Pomos or Pakhyammos. The road which is very pleasant and in some places runs by the coast. It is being replanned and widened so this area will become more attractive and accessible to tourists.

MINOUSA is to the right of the road and before getting there, you go through **MAGOUNDA.** These are old mining areas which date back thousands of years. **LIMNI Mine** was the last to close and was operating until not so long ago.

ARGAGA is reached by another turning to the right along the main road. It is an

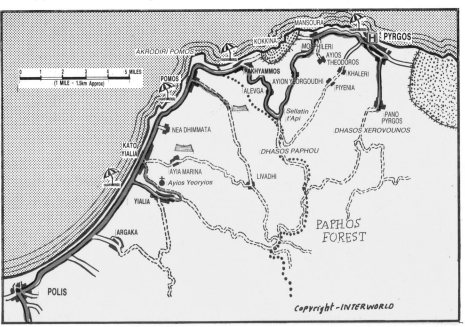

Pomos Beach.

125

agricultural centre with some 450 inhabitants. The old church has been rebuilt recently. A truck road will take you inland into empty but beautiful countryside and to the old site of the monastery of *Ayios Merkourios* to the south east.

YIALIA is about a mile inland and was a Turkish village but since the inhabitants left, the Greek refugees from the north, have administered their land. It is an agricultural centre and, as with the surrounding area, is known for the mild winter climate and thus for the early production of fruit and vegetables. The village is built on the hills and in the valley and provides beautiful views. Although a Frankish presence is apparent, the church of *Ayios Cornuto* is of a rare shape.

Above Top: Part of Pyrgos town. *Top* Pyrgos beach is not perfect but it is not bad either for the few visitors who decide to come this far.

126

KATO YIALIA (Lower Yialia). Just to the northwest of Yialia and close to the beach. It is mainly a fishing village from people who came from **Ayia Marina,** inland to the east. There are some good beaches around here. The forest to the east of this area was largely burnt in 1974 by the Turkish invading forces, but as soon as the fires died, a programme of replanting was started with great success.

POMOS (some 500 inhabitants), a fishing village but also becoming a tourist centre with a good beach and a couple of tavernas by the beach (summer only). Further to the north is *Pomos Point* where the coast is rocky but extremely lovely.

A truck road to the south east towards the Pomos Dam and down the gorge of the river *Livadhi* reveals beautiful scenery. Near the dams are the ruins of an old monastery but the church of *Khrysopateritissa* dated 16th century survived and is of some interest because of its icons. A tortuous journey will take you towards Stavros tis Psokas.

PAKHYAMMOS a pretty settlement with a very nice beach. To the north is the Turkish occupied enclave of Kokkina and photography is not permitted here.

PYRGOS is on the other side of the enclave and access is difficult as the coastal road cannot be used due to the objections of the occupying Turkish authorities. But a road has been made going around the enclave and then to Pyrgos through the western edges of the Paphos Forest. A trip to this area would be enjoyed mostly by nature lovers as there is not much else to be seen.

A small fishing harbour has been established and together with the small hotel it attracts more visitors now, either on day trips or short stays.

Sir Samuel Baker in his book "Cyprus as I saw it" wrote in 1879:

"Pyrgos — This is one of the wildest parts of Cyprus. There is a village but the position is simply marked by the presence of one building above the sea-beach which has been a depot for the span and poles of pine . . ."

Pomos Point coastline.

General view of Pyrgos, an ideal quiet place for those wishing to get away from civilization.

ROUTE FG-2
POLIS TO LYSO

East of Polis is the village of **PETHA-LOUSA** situated south of **KINOUSA**. This area is the extension of the mines to the north as mentioned in route F-1. But it is believed that it was the area where the miners lived as many rock cut and other tombs were found, also the remains of an old village. A block of stone with an inscription in Cypriote writing was also found here. The church of *Panayia Khorteni* contains an old tomb and some frescoes.

From here a truck road will take you to **Lyso** to the southeast. However, for comfortable driving it is better to reach Lyso from the main road, turn left just outside Polis on the Polis-Paphos road. The countryside is beautiful.

STENI — a small agricultural village. To the northwest after the settlement of *Ayios Isidoros* is an area called **Myrmikoph** and the ruins of an old 13th century monastery of *Khrysolakouma*. It is believed that it was built on the site of an ancient temple. The monastery was abandoned in 1821 when its last abbot was hanged by the Turkish authorites.

PERISTERONA / MELADIOU small villages of no great importance.

LYSO about 500 inhabitants, but once a much larger village with over 1000 people, of whom many emigrated abroad, mainly to Australia and Africa. Those who remained are some of the most energetic people of Paphos and the village is listed as one of the cleanest and well kept of all the Cypriot villages. It is fascinating to wander around the beautiful village with its old houses and narrow streets. There is a folk museum where old objects of domestic use are exhibited, like the spinning wheels, the baking of bread etc. A small cafe is situated behind the museum, in the courtyard. But a visit to the Kafenion will also provide you with refreshments.

The church of *Panayia Khryseleousa* is of medieval origin and a coat of arms of the Latin period is to be seen. Some parts of the church show a certain Gothic influence and there are some icons of interest. Below

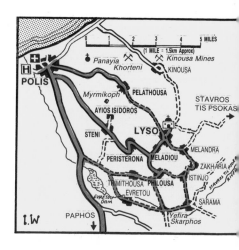

the church is the *Vrysi* (water fountain) with continuous cool, running water. Once Lyso was famous for the amount of water which was available all the year round.

In the areas of Trimithousa, to Maladiou and here at Lyso, traces of old habitation and ancient tombs have been found.

From here you may reach **Stavros tis Psokas** (but the road is difficult), or go south east and explore the area which provides beautiful scenery with views of high mountains, valleys, gorges, vineyards, carob and almond trees and in some places citrus, but the driving is hard. It includes the villages of **MELOUNDA, ZUKHARIA, The Junction of Istinjo, PHILOUSA,** and **TRIMITHOUSA** which although of no great importance, played some part in the islands' history during the Turkish occupation when a well-to-do Turk Giaour Imam, raged at the repressive measures against the peasants from the Turkish governor of Nicosia and in 1833 started a revolt which spread throughout Paphos and for many months he was in control of the district but, the revolution came to a tragic end.

LYSO FESTIVAL — August

This event started in 1985 by a small group of villagers both for the village and those living abroad as a get-together. Now it has become an annual event. Not only villagers from Australia and South Africa come back to their roots but it attracts numerous other visitors.

Above: The Medieval Church of Panayia at Lyso. *Below:* The southern side of the Church and the water fountains, once a centre of activity and meeting place of the villagers.

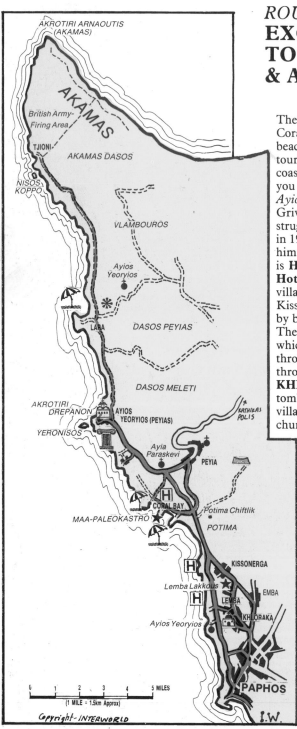

ROUTE H –
EXCURSIONS TO CORAL BAY & AKAMAS

There are two roads leading to Coral Bay — the most popular beach of Paphos and the largest tourist village. One is the new coastal road. Half way to the left you will see the new church of *Ayios Yeoryios* where General Grivas, leader of EOKA in the struggle for independence, landed in 1954. The boat which brought him is kept here. Then to the left is **Helios Apts** and **Cynthiana Hotel,** to the right side, the villages of Khlorakas, Lemba and Kissonerga and all are surrounded by banana plantations.

The other route is the old road which is as pleasant. You go through the town of Paphos and through the northern part of **KHLORAKAS** village. Ancient tombs were found here. By the village square is the large modern church and the 13th century church of *Panayia Khryseleousa,* one of the rarest of its type in Cyprus, similar to that of Ayios Theodosios at Adhelia. Modern holiday homes, some of them occupied by British families, have been built on the south side of the village with commanding views of the sea. **LEMBA** — A small village where the Paphos Art College operates (see under activities). Recent excavations have brought to light the remains of very early civilisations going back to the 4th millenium BC. This is a very important discovery giving clear evidence that life has existed in Paphos from that time.

KISSONERGA. Was built in the middle ages as an agricultural estate, although remains have been found of even earlier civilisations, a Byzantine watch tower and church in ruins is outside the village. It is a centre for banana plantations and to the south is Cynthiana hotel.

Between the village and Coral Bay, towards the northern side, close to the old bridge, is a site called *Potima* and in the middle ages Fossil remains of **Hippopotamus Minutus** were found. It is very interesting as fossils of this pigmy hippopotamus were found only in Cyprus, Malta and Crete. When the fossils were discovered the local people thought that they were remains of Christian Martyrs who were persecuted by the Romans and called the place *Ayii Planentes* (discovered Saints).

Above: Ayios Yeoryios Church. Once an isolated modern church is now surrounded by modern hotels.
Below: A beautiful sunset as seen from the Helios Bay Apartments, along the coastal road to Coral Bay.

131

LEMBA – LAKKOUS to the south-western outskirts of Lemba village, a large chalcolithic site; the most important of the western coast of Paphos c. 3000-2500 BC. Circular houses have been discovered together with burial places and objects discovered include a beautiful necklace, a rich variety of pottery, limestone female figurines and other items. The place is fenced.

KISSONERGA MOSPHILIA & MYLOUTHKIA to the north of Lemba and close to the outskirts of Kissonerga and near to Lemba-Lakkous. The first of the chalcolithic period; finds include female terracotta figurines and red type pottery. The latter is of less importance dating to the end of the Neolithic beginning of Chalcolithic periods. Both places are fenced.

Above: Students discuss their work at the college.
Below: Another assessment of work by Artist Stass Paraskos.

Above: A reconstructed circular house at Lemba-Lakkous. The area has been established as very important archaeologically. *Below:* The ancient site of Maa-Paleokastro. *(Courtesy Cyprus Museum).*

MAA-PALEOKASTRO, an important site due to its position, served as a military outspot for the Greek settlers (c.1230-1200 BC) arriving in great numbers.

CORAL BAY

This lovely area is developing as a tourist attraction and holiday village, with houses owned by locals as well as many British, who have established a small but well organised community. There are several tavernas here where one can simply order drinks, or have a good, freshly-cooked meal. The sandy beaches are clean and ideal for children and non-swimmers, since the water is very shallow and therefore very safe. Sea sports facilities are available in these very popular Paphos beaches.

Together with the nearby CORALLIA BAY the area has developed into a tourist village and villas, apartments and a planned hotel complex have transformed the whole place.

At the far end and between the two major bays, on a peninsular just beyond the taverna, stand the ruins of **Maa-Paleokastro,** an early Bronze Age settlement which was fortified. It is also believed that the area was a major disembarkation point

133

of the new settlers arriving from Greece. The area has been fenced off since excavation work is continuing, although visitors may enter if work is in progress and the gates open. Huge stones, which were part of the fortification, are still visible.

> For better or worse the Coral Bay area is rapidly changing character. Gone is the peace and quiet of the few residential houses and the beaches which were a paradise for the bathers. Now more accommodation has been built, holiday homes, shops, tavernas, a couple of large hotel complexes, even a small marina. It seems, one cannot stop progress . . .

Coming back onto the main road and turning left we reach the picturesque village of **PEYIA,** which has a lovely church and some interesting little houses which are very well kept. The village is of Byzantine origin.

The view of the coastline from the Church is wonderful. South of the road after leaving Peyia there is a modern church, built on the site of an old monastery, which stopped functioning in 1788 AD. The church of Ayia Paraskevi is dedicated to Panayia tou Zalajon, the curer of varicose veins.

From the upper part of the village one can enjoy excellent views of Coral Bay below. Tavernas and cafes are open until the early hours.

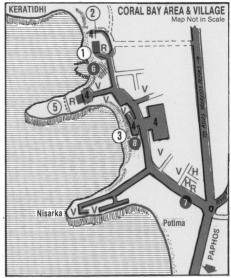

(1)	**CORALLIA BAY/BEACH** & Windsurfing Facilities	(R) **RESTAURANT**
(2)	**CAMPING AREA (No Facilities)**	(H) **HOTEL**
(3)	**CORAL BAY/MAIN BEACH**	(V) **VILLAS-HOUSES**
(4)	**PARKING SPACES**	(Please Note: Some
(5)	**MAA-PALEOKASTRO** (ANCIENT SITE)	new Accommodation is planned for the
(6)	**LEPTOS HOTEL** Complex and Marina	future)
(7)	**TOURIST VILLAGE**	
(8)	**Other hotels under planning or construction)**	

Below: Coral Bay in its much quieter days. It gets more crowded in the months of July and August. *(Courtesy Elpi Paskalis)*

Above and *below:* Two views of main Coral Bay beaches. Despite changes in the area in general with new hotels and private accommodation, the beaches are not affected, they just attract more bathers.

AYIOS YEORYIOS

Going through banana plantations one reaches a small settlement dominated by the small church of **Ayios Yeoryios, Peyias.**

There is a taverna and a guest house where one can stay when exploring the surrounding area and there is a good beach for swimming below the village. From the top of the hill there is a view of the small bay, which was used by the Romans for swimming and fishing. There are fishing boats which give an extra attraction. The small island of Ayios Yeoryios (600 feet long and 60 feet wide) can be seen about 500 feet off-shore. On the island are the remains of what is thought to be a Neolithic settlement. Close to the settlement of Ayios Yeoryios are early Christian churches and houses. Floor remains and mosaics and the main Basilica is open to the public during working hours and they are worth visiting. Below the cliff and above the fishing harbour and the beach, caves have been cleared and are open to the public. Burial Chambers were carved in the rock.

Above: Part of the remains of ancient Basilica at Cape Drepanum (Ayios Yeoryios Peyias).

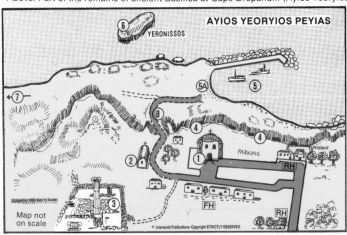

AYIOS YEORYIOS PEYIAS

YERONISSOS

(1) MODERN CHURCH OF AYIOS YEORYIOS
(2) OLD CHAPEL OF AYIOS YEORYIOS
(3) EARLY CHRISTIAN BASILICA (Fenced)
(4) TOMBS & CHAMBERS Below Cliffs
(5) SMALL FISHING HARBOUR
(5A) Small Beach with shingles
(6) YERONISSOS ISLAND
(7) TO KANTARKASTI CAVES
(8) Truck Road - suitable to most cars
(FH) FISHERMEN'S HOMES
(RH) RESTAURANT-CAFETERIA.
(A) BASIC ACCOMMODATION

PARKING

Map not on scale

136

CAPE DREPANUN – Originally a Roman town and harbour, the area of Ayios Yeoryios Peyias became an important place to the Christians during the 6th century AD. Three basilicas were erected here. The main one was a 3 aisled church; excavations carried out show the extent of the buildings including a spacious baptistry, parts of corinthian columns and geometric mosaic floors. The area is fenced but you can observe it from the sides.

Caves which are cut into rock below the cliffs can be explored but be aware of falling rocks. There's still no information of their actual use.

Right: The dominating church of Ayios Yeoryios Peyias. *Below:* A panoramic view of the harbour and the island of Yeronissos. The area is ideal for snorkelling and fishing.

KANTARKASTOI CAVES

These are sea caves which can be reached either by sea or land. By land you may go there by descending a narrow path from the church of Ayios Yeoryios. The caves are about half a mile from the church to the East. You can take the path which goes near the sea and after walking for three-quarters of an hour you will reach them. These are the only good sea caves to be seen in Cyprus. The caves are not all together and you have to walk from one place to another to see them all. Some of the caves are deep and the sea enters. Some of them communicate, the water entering one and coming out of another. The colours of the inside of the caves are wonderful — green and violet changing in the light which reflects from the water. The legend of these caves is that at the time of the Saracen raids the people of the village of Peyia ran to the mountains and forests in order to save their lives. Once they returned to the sea they saw many rocks in a row on the shore front. Then they realised that Ayios Yeoryios had protected them from the Saracens (Arabs) by throwing these rocks at the invaders. For better exploration you may ask a local fisherman from Ayios Yeoryios to take you there by boat for a small fee.

The area can also be reached from a small tourist complex about 1km before reaching Ayios Yeoryios.

GORGE OF THE PEYIA FOREST

Beyond Ayios Yeoryios Peyias is a short but fascinating Gorge, called the *"Gorge of Peyia Forest"* or the *Gorge of the Eggs* unknown to most people and unique in Cyprus. It is situated to the west of Peyia. *'A patch of nature that is so far untouched'* said the main explorer the archaeologist David Pearlman, a resident of Paphos who runs "EXALT" (Excursion Alternatives).

Prehistoric evidence plus Greek-Roman tombs show that the area was occupied throughout antiquity.
It is difficult, if not impossible to reach the Gorge except for fully experienced hikers; trips are organised by a few specialists including EXALT (Tel. 243803) and are very rewarding.

NOTE: The gorge is completely unprotected, so visitors are urged not to litter or write on the gorge walls.

Below: Kantarkastoi Caves. *Right:* The fascinating Gorge of the Peyia Forest. *(Courtesy David Pearlman (Exalt Travel Ltd).)*

LARA

For the most adventurous a trip to Lara will provide empty sandy beaches for swimming, away from the crowds. However, to get there on the narrow twisting roads you need a good car. Do not drive after heavy rain (this applies mainly to winter visitors) as you may stick in mud. Also be aware of British army trucks which use the road on the way to Akamas for exercises. The road is not surfaced and is full of stones, some which are large.

Lara offers exotic surroundings. The area is also well-known for its turtle breeding.

The Turtles of Lara

Unique in the mediterranean, this isolated and deserted part of Cyprus attracted the **Green Turtle** in the past. Some beaches have been taken by the Ministry of Fisheries who are trying hard to protect this small remaining colony of the species as more and more tourists venture into this area.

> **We request all our readers to respect the Turtles and should you see any stray turtles, please inform the officials. They must be preserved at all cost, so everyone's help is vital.**

Above: The Lara Beach with Turtles nest. Yes, the beach is nice, but the Turtles *(see below)* are more important and must be respected.

DEEP INTO AKAMAS PENINSULA

Driving further away the road becomes more stoney but the forest of Akamas is beautiful. The beaches below are inviting and some of the coast is rocky with small islands — the largest being Koppo Island, which is interesting for its shape. The truck road ends at a small bay called **TJIONI**. The area around here is unfortunately closed when the British army practices, but this does not often happen.

The fascinating aspect of this place is a weather-beaten column which sticks out of the water and is believed to be a mooring column. The ruins of a pier (mainly rock now) can be seen nearby. The Romans had a port here and one wonders if the lost city of Akamas (named after the Athenian Akamanthus who founded it after the Trojan War) is either buried nearby or submerged under water. Archaeologists are still looking for the lost royal city. In this area, beware of unexploded shells. Climbing up the mountain from here is a very poor truck route which one should attempt **with a Landrover only.** On the top of the mountains you can see the remains of British anti-aircraft installations from the Second World War. The forest is superb and the surrounding views wonderful. The truck road will take you over the other side of the mountains to the Fontana Amoroza area and then to Baths of Aphrodite Latchi and Polis.

Above: The regular inhabitants of Akamas, the Cypriot Goats enjoy their freedom. *Below:* Exploration with a Land Rover. The truck, road leading to the sea shows the sheer size of the area. The bay by the coast is that of Tjioni, site of ancient settlements, but also where the British army exercise with live ammunition.

Above: The Far end point of Akamas peninsula.
Below: A picturesque view of Akamas coastline
(Courtesy David Pearlman/Exalt Travel Ltd.)

There is a strong debate regarding the future of Akamas some want it to remain as it is at present, some propose a very limited and controlled opening to the public, others, perhaps with more vested interest, propose the creation of more open tourist areas.

We invite our readers to tell us what they think and we promise to make their opinions and suggestions known to the authorities.

AKAMAS — Summary

This area is mysterious, not only to foreign visitors but also to locals. It is only visited by fishermen, hunters, the British army for exercises and some adventurous tourists. It is more or less in its natural state. However, this will change soon, as a coastal road is planned all the way up to the Baths of Aphrodite and tourist establishments will be erected. However, there is now a growing opposition which prefers the area to remain in its natural state and to be declared a National Park. You can help by expressing your views, so if you are a lover of nature, explore it now, as Hogarth did in 1887-88 who wrote:

"It is a sterile corner of Cyprus, thickly covered with scrub, abounding in deep gullies and bold rock formations, the central spine being broken into bold peaks or miniature table mountains; here and there in a tiny valley is a cultivated patch, but nine tenths of the district produces nothing but game ..."

Although the area is now uninhabited, there are many signs that this was not always so. At the headland of Cape Drepano by Ayios Yeoryios, Roman and Byzantine settlements were discovered; inland, signs of ruined Byzantine churches in the forest of Meleti, together with rock cut tombs of unknown origin and further up at Lara and the area of Konon there is an abandoned, ancient settlement. This and the church of Ayios Konon can be seen just under 1 mile inland amongst the pines. The bay of Tjioni used to be a Roman settlement, most submerged under water now.

CHAPTER 4

WHAT PAPHOS OFFERS!

Well, Paphos in simple language offers a bit of everything. Although it lacks some modern facilities, such as golf, horse riding etc. Paphos is a paradise of beautiful and contrasting scenery, fascinating coastal seascapes, historical monuments and very friendly and hospital people.

In the following pages we will concentrate on the most important landmarks which make Paphos "a special place".

Sunset over Coral Bay.

ACTIVITIES

WATERSPORTS: These have become very popular in Paphos and can be enjoyed mainly by the main hotels, large beaches of Pissouri, Paphos, Coral Bay and Latchi —Polis area.

They include windsurfing, waterskiing, parachuting, boating, sailing, fishing etc. When choosing, make sure that they are licensed and safe.

FISHING EXPEDITIONS: Some fishing can be done inland in reservoirs after obtaining a permit from the fisheries department. Fishing in the sea along the coast is without restrictions. Some hotels organise individual or small party expeditions around Coral Bay, Lara, Akamas, and Latchi. You may approach some fishermen in Paphos and Latchi harbour who for a fee may take you fishing.

SEA CRUISES: Mainly during the summer months there are regular boat trips and cruises for a few hours or the whole day. These can be very enjoyable. Information can be obtained from the harbour pier.

UNDERWATER EXPLORATION: Paphos, over the last few years has become a centre for professional and amateur divers from all over Western Europe. The excellent climate of Paphos, the facilities of the harbour, the hard work of local people and professional British divers who are now residents of Paphos, have contributed to this popular expansion. The **CYDIVE** centre is situated close to the harbour and has its own premises at Poseidonos Avenue — Kato Paphos — Tel. 234271. The club is called *DIVERS DEN* where divers and friends meet for a drink or a chat also for slide shows, barbeques or to plan their next excursion. CYDIVE is organised to a high degree of proficiency and has highly qualified and expert instructors who will undertake to supervise other divers. They have internationally accepted qualifications such as the BS-AC and ASA. They also teach groups and individuals. The club is very well equipped with suites and all necessary equipment, boats and landrovers. Any visitor to Paphos can enjoy the shores and coast which provide excellent marine life, some old and new wrecks, signs of submerged ruins, caves and valleys. Underwater photography shows an abundance of colourful marine life with subjects such as octopus, moray, eels, large groupers, soldier fish, sponges, gorgonians, sea shells etc.

Sea Explorers of Cydive with an "Aphorae". *(Courtesy Mark Caney/Cydive Ltd.)*

Above: Panayia to Sindi abandoned monastery and the river Xeros *(Courtesy David Pearlman/Exalt Travel Ltd).*
Below: Anneka Rice explores the seabed of Paphos *(Courtesy Mark Caney/Cydive Ltd).*

HINTERLAND EXPLORATIONS:

The wonder and mystery of Western Cyprus — the Paphos district can be explored with EXALT (Excursion Alternatives) Tel. (06) 243803, Fax: (06) 246167 — based in Kato Paphos.

They are organised by archaeologist and explorer David Pearlman and a professional team of individuals provide off-the-beaten track hiking and jeep expeditions.

Destinations are mainly to far away places such as newly discovered archaeological sites; the breathtaking Gorge of Peyia Forest; Thalassines Spilies (sea caves); Isolated and abandoned old monasteries and chapels; Uninhabited villages; Primitive sheepfolds and shepherd haunts.

Great care is taken not to disturb or damage the environment and to preserve this wilderness.

The groups programme caters for a variety of special interests such as Archaeology, Architecture, Bird-watching, Ethnography, Geology and Trekking and attracts people from many parts of the world who regard Paphos as a unique place for exploration in the Mediterranean.

Above: Exploring the Paphos Countryside.
Above right: The fascinating Gorge of Peyia *(both courtesy David Pearlman/Exalt Ltd).*
Below: A fisherman with his catch.

TENNIS: Some hotels provide tennis facilities, mainly for residents. There is a tennis court in the public gardens near the 28th October Square which is open to all, also at the Plaz area.

HUNTING: This is very popular in Cyprus and Paphos mountains provide excellent hunting places. Hunting is permitted in special areas only and at certain periods and a special licence is required.

PHOTOGRAPHY: Paphos is an ideal place for landscape photography. Local photographic shops provide all well known films and can also develop and print within 24 hours. Photography, however, as in all other countries is prohibited in areas near military camps and around Pachiamnos and Pyrgos close to areas occupied by the Turkish army.

For keen photographers, make sure that you are well stocked with "professional" films and by exploring the countryside you will find a lot of material. But please note that in the summer months the atmosphere is hazy.

SPORTS: Paphos has two football

teams; and nearly all matches attract good crowds.

In athletics you can train or participate with local athletes. There are two stadiums with limited athletic facilities.

SOCIETIES: Two International societies, LYONS and ROTARY clubs have branches in Paphos and regular meetings take place at the Paphos Beach Hotel.

PAINTING: The clear colours, the contrasting landscapes and seascapes, the mountains and valleys the churches and villages, all provide the ideal material for landscape painting. With the establishment of an Art College *(see page 132)* and an Art Gallery "Kyknos" in Kato Paphos and a main one planned in the main town, Paphos is rapidly becoming a centre for artists.

In Paphos, live and work some of the most important artists in Cyprus such as the sculptor, Andy Hatziadamos and Kypros Perdios and the painters Andreas Charalambides, George Kotsonis, Christos Foukarus, Costas Economou, Andreas Makariou, Rinos Stephani and Stass Paraskos.

Above: A studio of an artist at Exo Vrysi — Ktima.
Below: Ruins of an abandoned settlement (village). The mountainous region of Paphos is an ideal place to explore, paint or photograph such abandonment places. *(Courtesy David Pearlman/Exalt Ltd.)*

THE BEACHES OF PAPHOS

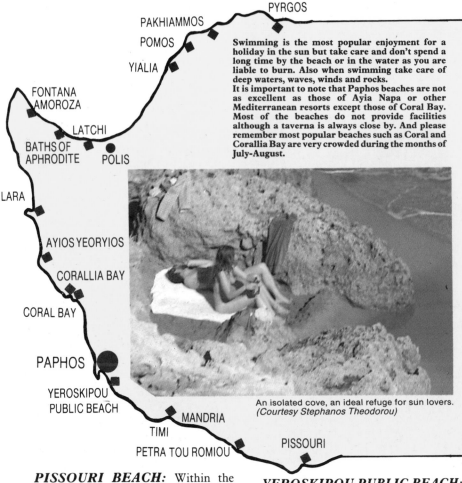

PYRGOS

PAKHIAMMOS

POMOS

YIALIA

FONTANA AMOROZA

LATCHI

BATHS OF APHRODITE

POLIS

LARA

AYIOS YEORYIOS

CORALLIA BAY

CORAL BAY

PAPHOS

YEROSKIPOU PUBLIC BEACH

MANDRIA

TIMI

PETRA TOU ROMIOU

PISSOURI

Swimming is the most popular enjoyment for a holiday in the sun but take care and don't spend a long time by the beach or in the water as you are liable to burn. Also when swimming take care of deep waters, waves, winds and rocks.

It is important to note that Paphos beaches are not as excellent as those of Ayia Napa or other Mediterranean resorts except those of Coral Bay. Most of the beaches do not provide facilities although a taverna is always close by. And please remember most popular beaches such as Coral and Corallia Bay are very crowded during the months of July-August.

An isolated cove, an ideal refuge for sun lovers.
(Courtesy Stephanos Theodorou)

PISSOURI BEACH: Within the Bay of Pissouri, mainly sandy with some pebbles but deep in places. Facilities provided by the hotel and tavernas.

PETRA TOU ROMIOU: Aphrodites Birthplace. Mainly sandy bays with pebbles and some rocks. Be careful of deep areas and under-currents. The tourist pavilion a short distance away is ideal for a meal afterwards.

MANDRIA: A partly sandy beach which is open to southern winds.

TIMI: Two beaches, one partly sandy with a taverna-restaurant and a place for camping.

YEROSKIPOU PUBLIC BEACH: To the east of Paphos, with changing cabins and showers, restaurant-cafeteria-grass lawn. The beach is a mixture of sand, shingles and seaweeds. Many seasports are available.

WITHIN PAPHOS: Small stretches of beach, most popular in front of the hotels. The breakwaters now provide small coves and better facilities than before. Also near the lighthouse. Do not expect long beaches in the Paphos town area as most of the coast is rocky.

CORAL BAY: The most popular during the summer, however empty in

148

early morning and late afternoon. Nice sandy and shallow waters. Cafes-restaurants and facilities.

CORALLIA BAY: Next to Coral Bay, good sandy beach, but can change after a heavy winter. Centre for windsurfing and other sports. Restaurant, shops, showers and a new hotel.

AYIOS YEORYIOS: More of an idylic little harbour than a beach, but can provide some bathing. Cafeterias and restaurant.

LARA: Excellent sandy beaches mainly empty due to bad road connections. We urge you not to use it due to the turtles. However, if you do, please take great care.

FONTANA AMOROZA: Isolated coastline of unique beauty with small coves with sand and pebbles; difficult to reach.

BATHS OF APHRODITE: Mainly pebble but with some sand, excellent clear waters, small coves and good rock formations. The tourist pavilion offers changing and shower facilities and excellent fish.

LATCHI AREA: Long stretches of sandy beaches with some pebbles at places to the east and west of the harbour. Numerous tavernas provide meals and refreshments.

POLIS: Long beaches along the bay close to the town. The best way to reach the beach is through the camping site.

YIALIA AREA: Main road runs along the beach (separated at places with houses). However, the long beaches are mainly pebbled and not always clean.

POMOS-PAKHYAMMOS: At places are some small sheltered bays with empty beaches. At Pakhyammos the beach is long and mainly sandy and empty.

PYRGOS: Just before entering the village. An excellent beach with a taverna and showers.

Within the village by the hotel Tolon, a long pebbled beach; restaurants and tavernas. An ideal spot for the townsfolk to relax.

Above: Beach activity. *Right:* Coral Bay. *Below:* One of the beaches near Latchi area.

SHOPPING

SHOPPING is part of every visitor's holiday enjoyment, and Paphos, like every other tourist centre, provides a large selection of items to suit everyone. However be careful of cheap imitations which are produced in some Asian countries. Although most of the shops are Europeanised in both looks and attitudes and their prices are displayed, you may care to try the old eastern tradition of bargaining.

Most of the shopkeepers are owners thus providing a friendly and very personal service, some may even offer you coffee or a drink. Most of them speak English. Whether you shop for souvenirs, or you want clothes, toiletries, you will find that most of the items are available. Good handicrafts, pottery and jewellery are ideal items to purchase, but search for the good shops.

FOOD. For fresh fruit, vegetables, meat and fish, visit the Paphos public market. Other shops are around the town and close to most hotels and in Polis. They will supply the vegetables, fruit and food provisions mainly needed by those in self catering accommodation.

When you do shopping, do it in a leisurely way. It is best to go either in the early morning or late afternoon when it is cooler. **Shopping hours** vary, but due to midday siesta most of the shops open between 8am-1pm and 4pm-7pm (in winter there is a shorter lunch break and they close earlier at night). Saturday is a half day. In some tourist areas shops are open longer hours.

Above right: Woven items ideal for decorations or table covers.
Below: A souvenir shop at Yeroskipos with baskets, delights etc.

EATING OUT

EATING OUT, whether you have made fullboard or halfboard arrangements with your hotel, is a must, not only for tasting the delicious local specialities but also to enjoy the atmosphere and taste the various wines of Cyprus.

Apart from the Hotels and Apartments which have their own restaurant and welcome visitors, you can enjoy a nice Cypriot meal at the various Tavernas, Kebab Houses and Fish Restaurants which are all over the town and the harbour. Most of them offer local decor and Greek atmosphere and in the summer you eat outside in the fresh air. Most meals are Cypriot but if you prefer steaks or simple food like an omelette, do not hesitate to ask even if it isn't on the menu. They will be very pleased to provide you with a meal to your own taste.

In recent years, more diverse eating places provide Chinese, Indian, Italian and other specialities thus catering for all tastes.

In the surrounding villages more tavernas have been established providing some true local village atmosphere.

. CAFETERIAS, SALAD BARS AND BARS. These provide refreshments, coffee, drinks and beers but also provide some meals and serve sandwiches, ice cream and cakes. Many of them have their chairs and tables on a wide pavement by the road and you can sit there as long as you wish to watch the world go by.

PUBS. These mainly try to promote the British pub atmosphere. They are pleasant to visit and there are restrictions to their opening hours, some can go up to 2am. You will find all local and International drinks including many whisky brands, gin and probably a wider selection of beers than the two lager brands which are the main ones served in the island.

> For your eating you may try the **MEZE.** This is a collection of either fish or meat appetizers including cheeses, salads and dips and are selected from the various dishes which we describe below and and some can also be served as individual meals.

In a good Cypriot taverna or restaurant you are always welcome to go into the kitchen and discuss what you wish to eat and if you wish to enjoy a fish meal, you may be shown a selection from which you can choose your own.

Generally, Eating Out in Paphos is a real enjoyment, something which leaves most of the visitors fully satisfied.

People enjoying a nice relaxing evening in one of Paphos' many establishments.

ENTERTAINMENT

Since Paphos became a major tourist centre, various pubs, tavernas and other places of entertainment have mushroomed, mainly in Kato Paphos, close to the hotels and the harbour, as mentioned in the previous page. For the most energetic there are the various places of entertainment.

NIGHTCLUBS / BOUZOUKIA: These places provide Greek music and singing, mainly live and you can participate in the singing and dancing. They are mainly open from about 11pm up to the early hours. There are a number of them in Paphos. You may also find during the summer a cabaret night club where various shows take place. If in doubt, check with your hotel personnel, they will be glad to advise you where to go.

Some of the **tavernas** which provide eating may also have occasional evenings of bouzouki music, singing and folk dancing during the summer.

HOTEL ENTERTAINMENT: During the tourist season, the hotels and some of the apartments have various evening functions such as beach parties, or nights of Greek Cypriot folk dancing, singing, eating, wine tasting, etc. You are free to go around the various hotels and check the programmes and attend their functions. You may even attend one of the many annual Balls given by various clubs and organisations of Paphos (dinner and dance) which occur throughout the year mainly in hotels.

Occasionally hotels organise various special events such as beauty contests, special dances etc.

DISCOS: For the young and most energetic there are a number of discos which are now of good quality and presentation. Here the young local people mix with the young visitors and generally the atmosphere is friendly and happy.

Nightlife in Paphos is simple but exciting to both young and adults.

Above and Below: Scenes of CYPRIOT NIGHT entertainment. This is a regular event, at least once weekly in most hotels and other large establishments, not only for the resident guests but also for everyone. These nights apart from the traditional dancing and music, also provide an excellent cuisine which is either meze or buffet.

FESTIVALS & EVENTS

There are a number of popular festivals which attract interest and create fun for all the family. There are also some less important local activities and festivals which are not mentioned here. If you are interested, watch out for local advertising. *The major festivals are:*

PAPHOS CARNIVAL: This is something new to Paphos and it started in 1983 as a continuation of a very old tradition and in competition to the even larger carnival of Limassol. One of the masterminds of this event is the very progressive and well liked mayor of Paphos the late Mr. Agrotis. The carnival takes place during the weekend preceding Lent, with processions of floats, bands, the singing of songs, dancing etc. During the week children dress in various fancy costumes and visit their friends .to see if they can be recognised. Local organisations give dances.

ANTHESTIRIA: This is a flower festival, and has been well established in Paphos for many years. It is held at the beginning of May, with parades of chariots, participants are decorated with flowers using themes from the Greek mythology, tradition, nature etc. The event also includes, folk dancing and singing. The festival is thought to originate in a celebration for Aphrodite.

CATAKLYSMOS: The festival is held 50 days after Easter on a Sunday at Kato Paphos Harbour. There are water games of various kinds and much eating, singing and dancing. Stalls offer various homemade products. It is the celebration of the "Flood".

PAMPAPHIA: This is a new and well established folk festival which takes place during the first week of August. There are parades, bands (occasionally you may enjoy the band of the Royal Highlanders). Greek folk singing and dancing, agricultural and art exhibitions and many gastronomic specialities, using the art of Cypriot cooking. This festival is not annual.

WINE FESTIVAL (Dionysia): This is held during the last week of August or the first week of September at Stroumbi village, one of the Paphos wine centres. Local wine tasting and plentiful free wine are available. There is folk dancing, singing, and local food specialities. Also exhibitions of agricultural products, embroidery and lace are held.

OTHER FESTIVALS include the **AYIOS NEOPHYTOS FAIR** at the monastery, September 27th and 28th; **ANCIENT DRAMA FESTIVAL** at the open ancient theatre (ODEON) with performances of ancient drama or comedies by students or professional theatrical groups during June-July; **LYSSOS VILLAGE** Festival; **RESI** Festival at Kallepia; **Archaeological Symposium** at Kissonerga and Kouklia; Religious **FAIR** (Panygiri) at Khrysorroyiatissa Monastery.

The Carnival of Paphos.

Information about these and other festivals and accurate dates can be obtained from the Tourist Information Office in Paphos Tel: (06) 232841.

Above: A colourful scene from the annual Paphos Flower Festival *(Courtesy Stephanos Theodorou).*
Below: One of the numerous Paphos folklore festivals.

THE VINEYARDS OF PAPHOS

Vineyards in Paphos are as old as its history. They were and still are the backbone of the economy of the district and villagers take much pride in their product. But the cultivation of vineyards until recently was done in primitive ways and reaching the various vineyards on the slopes of the hills was difficult. However, existing truck roads are now wide and other special truck roads have been constructed. Grants were given to the villagers and new vineyards were planned with better table grapes and better wine producing grapes. The cultivation is also done in a professional way, thus increasing production. '

In the months of August and early September, the countryside is full of people collecting the grapes, transporting them from the vineyards into baskets on the back of donkeys to the lorries which then transport them to the wineries. Some of the grape juice is spilled on the roads making them slippery, so take care when driving.

The main winery in Paphos is that of SODAP at Poseidonos Avenue.

PAPHOS REGIONAL WINERIES

These new wineries have been established in the areas of grape production and they take the utmost care in processing the grapes. Some of these regional wineries include those of Khrysorroyiatissa Monastery and the nearby Ambelitis wines of the Statos area close to Ayia Moni, the old monastic settlement. The area by itself is very interesting to explore.

Above: A Paphian Winery. *(Vouni Panayia Winery)*
Below: Collecting the grapes. *(Courtesy David Pearlman)*

THE PAPHOS VILLAGE

This does not differ much from other Cypriot villages but due to its physical isolation has created some special characteristics.

The Village House: Two rooms, one next to the other, formed the traditional house. One room has a large bed for the parents and smaller for the children. In some places, up to 10 people could be accommodated. The room was also used as a sitting room. Next to it the kitchen with an open fire, storing space and a dining table. Poorer families had one long room only, richer families more rooms, some for their animals, and a few big landowners with their larger farmhouses.

Village Characteristics: Every village has a church and one or more **"Kafenia"** (the coffee-shops or village pubs) mainly situated in the village square, where all the males gather to sip their coffee or brandy, to gossip and play cards or backgammon. A couple of shops to sell different goods are the basic industries of a blacksmith and a cobbler. Sunday is a day for church and afterwards for social gathering. A Wedding is the most important event of the village.

Local Panayiri (Fair): This occurs once or twice a year, mainly on the name day of the church saint. It starts with a pilgrimage to the saint, then a stroll around the fair to meet friends and buy local and other goods. It ends with a traditional feast of **souvla** (cooked meat on charcoal) or **"ofto"** (roast meat), with songs, dances, and drinking wine. This is a vital part of village life of religion, business and feasting. The main village occupation is agriculture. In fertile lands, they grow wheat, barley, beans, potatoes, onions, vegetables and fruit. Livestock is very important to all villagers, each family has its own poultry and pigs, mules or donkeys. Some own cattle as well.

Emigration to cities and abroad has left many villages without young people and many schools are closed. Old traditions are slowly disappearing and the attractions of modern civilisation, as in other parts of the world, are changing this life.

THE LAONA PROJECT
This project is geared to put back some life into Paphos villages and those mainly bordering the Akamas peninsula thus providing ecological tourism. The project is financed by the Leventis Foundation which is chaired by Constantine Leventis. It includes restoration of buildings, churches and the establishment of cultural centres.

Above and below: Two different and constructing Paphos villages.

157

THE COUNTRYSIDE

Fascinating valleys, productive trees, endless vineyards, wild flowers in the fields, all add to the Paphian charm — the ideal place to explore.

PRICKLY PEARS (Papoutsosika): A cactus type plant with large thick flat leaves. Once was used by the farmers as hedges to protect their fields from animals. The fruit produces colourful yellow flowers. When ripe it is eaten preferably when cold. The fruit is protected with thick skin and cactus type needles.

Prickly Pears

CAROB TREES: This is a rare survivor of the iron age. They grow in the countryside and require the minimum of care. Once they were called "the Black Gold" of Cyprus and were exported in great quantities from the harbour of Paphos mainly as animal feed. Carobs also produce tasty honey.

OLIVE TREES. This is a sacred tree in the Greek world. In Paphos it grows wild but also under supervision in fields. Both oil and olives are mainly consumed locally and form a main item of Cypriot diet.

Carob Trees

BANANAS: These are extensively grown in the Paphos district, are small but of excellent quality. The biggest enemy is frost which is rare in Paphos but great precaution is taken during winter. The banana trees require much care and lots of water. They are consumed in the island and also exported mainly to Arab countries.

CITRUS TREES: Orange and lemon production in Paphos has been expanded since the Turkish invasion and the occupation of the citrus growing areas of Morphou and Famagusta. The numerous dams erected in the Paphos district provide much needed water. Both lemons and oranges are of excellent quality and some are exported to British and other markets.

Olive Tree with shepherd *(Elpi Paskalis)*

ALMOND TREES: These are widely grown in most parts of the district and in many other parts of the island and due to the local and International demand of Almond Nuts, the product gives a reasonable revenue without requiring much attention.

Banana Trees *(Elpi Paskalis)*

158

The Almond trees are also liked for their blossoms during the spring, a sheer delight of beauty expressed by many poets and painted by many artists.

Lemons on a lemon tree.

Left Top: Almond tree in full blossom.
Above: An orange tree in glorious spring colourful field. *(Courtesy David Pearlman)*
Below: A girl collecting flowers in a colourful field. *(Courtesy Stephanos Theodorou).*

159

Above: Another Paphos mountain scene with an abandoned settlement — Spring time.
Below: The famous Paphos donkey, both very stubborn but also very patient. *(David Pearlman/Exalt Ltd.)*

160

USEFUL THINGS TO KNOW

Please note that some of the details quoted below and in previous pages change from time to time, therefore to be really sure that the information you have is correct and up to date you are advised to visit the:

**Tourist Information Office
3 Gladstone Street, Paphos
Tel:·232841**

Cyprus Head Office:
18 Th. Theodotou Street, P.O. Box 4535, Nicosia
Tel: (02) 443374

United Kingdom Office:
213 Regent Street, London W1R 8DA
Tel: 071-734 9822

TRAVELLING AROUND

If you have arranged an all inclusive tour, transfers from the airport to your hotel and vise a versa are arranged. However, there are regular taxi services which are very reasonably priced. Bus services also exist with connections to all towns and the airport.

TAXIS

Shared taxi services run frequently from town to town for a fixed price and most of them will take you to your destination address. Night services between towns are infrequent if they exist at all, so make sure to check for their last run. The Paphos to Limassol journey is still around CY£2.00. To travel around Paphos itself and the surrounding countryside, a taxi will be happy to take you anywhere at any time. The receptionist at your establishment will be happy to arrange a taxi for you. The main taxi services include: KARYDAS (232459), KYPROS (232376) KYRIAKOS (233181), MAKRIS (232538), NEA PAPHOS (232132). To Polis there is a regular service by Amoroza Bus (weekdays only) tel. 232459. To Pomos and Pyrgos via Polis is the Pyrgos bus (weekdays only).

BUSES

Bus services connect Paphos with the other towns via Limassol, they take longer for the journey although they charge less. They are operated by KEMEK Bus Company, Paphos office 234255. There is also a well organised bus service run by ALEPA Ltd which travels within the town, the harbour, the hotels and the ancient ruins and monuments from 6am-5pm daily (Sat. & Sun. 9am-5pm). Buses run every 30 minutes. There is also a regular service,

mainly in the summer to **Coral Bay** beach starting from Pervola bus station. The same company also runs services to various villages and tourist places such as Timi; Chloraka-Kissonerga-Coral Bay; Mesoyi-Tremithousa; Armoukonia; Emba-Tala; Yeroskipou. For up-to-date timetables telephone 234252 or 234410.

COACH TOURS

Sightseeing tours can be arranged by tourist agencies to visit important places in Paphos and further afield. They include Louis Tourist Agency, Aeolos Travel, Paradise Island Travel, Blue Sea Travel, Geko Tours, Salamis Tours.

CAR HIRE

If you do not have car-hire included in your all inclusive tour, you may hire a car in Paphos — any type of car for any period of time. However, one must remember there may be difficulties in hiring a car immediately in the busy months of July and August and prior arrangements are recommended. Please also check what an insurance policy covers. The main car hire firms are: PETSAS (235522); EUROP-CAR (234149); GECO TOURS (232347); HERTZ (233985); LOUIS TOURIST (233320); KLEOPAS (232508); SECURITY TRAVEL (233 278); BUDGET (235100).

BIKES & MOTORBIKES

This is an easy way to travel around especially for short distances and you can hire bikes or motorbikes from hotels or various tourist shops which specialise. Places for hiring also exist at Polis and Latchi.

Distances from Paphos Town to: in miles.

Peyia	10
Ayios Yeoryios	17
Tsada	7
Kathikas	16
Polis	25
Pomos	37
Lyso	31
Stroumbi	12
Phiti	20
Panayia	25
Galataria	24
Pendalia	22
Konia	2½
Episkopi	9½
Timi	6
Kedhares	25
Pretori	26
Kouklia	10
Ayios Neophitos	6
Petra tou Romiou	15
Stavros tis Psokas	32
Aphrodites Baths	30
Khrysorroyiatissa	27
Coral Bay	7
Paphos Airport	8
Larnaca Airport	91
Limassol	44
Larnaca	89
Platres	39
Nicosia	97

PLEASE REMEMBER

a) In Cyprus you drive on the same side of the road as in Britain.

b) Most petrol stations close Sat. afternoon, Sunday all day and Holidays, except for a few.

c) Parking meters exist in some parts of the town.

d) **Always, please take care of pedestrians, cyclists, and bad drivers. — Drive within the limits.**

THE WEATHER

Average max. day temperatures in Paphos (°Farenheit)

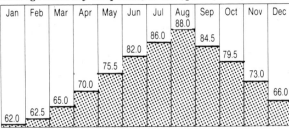

Jan	Feb	Mar	Apr	May	Jun	Jul	Aug	Sep	Oct	Nov	Dec
							88.0				
						86.0		84.5			
					82.0				79.5		
				75.5							
			70.0							73.0	
		65.0									66.0
62.0	62.5										

General climate: Paphos, surrounded on three sides by the sea has the mildest climate in Cyprus, where the summer heat is cooled with the breeze from the sea and the winters are fairly mild. Occasional clouds appear due to condensation. However, rain falls from time to time in the spring so do not be surprised if you find a few days of rain or bad weather in February or March even in April, although this is not regular and predictable. Early spring provides natural excitement with green fields, wild flowers, trees of oranges, lemon, almond in blossom and others with their extraordinary beauty. Migrating birds like swallows arrive and the whole countryside is completely different to that of the dry summer.

What to wear. From October to the end of March it is advisable to take some thicker clothes and cardigans as well, as it gets cold especially during the night when the sun has gone. During the winter months, when the wind blows from the north, it can get very cold. But in the Summer, light clothing and a thin cardigan for the night is all that is necessary as it is very hot.

MEDICAL CARE

It is always an upsetting experience when any visitor becomes unwell and needs medical attention. Medicine in most countries, not excluding Cyprus, is private and the visitor has to pay for services rendered though charges are low, ranging from £5-£10 for a visit at the doctor's surgery. Charges for home visits are a little higher and depend on the amount of medical treatment given. One can find medical care in most branches of medicine, though not all doctors are English speaking. There are, in the town, British qualified specialists and these are probably the best to seek advice from, bearing in mind the colloquial way in which the British express themselves. Their standard is amongst the highest on the island, in medicine and surgery.

The hospital service is government run and care is paid for by visitors. Some private clinics offer a better standard of nursing care.

MONEY MATTERS

As from October 1983 a new currency was introduced to replace the old decimal monetary system. The new currency is the **CENT**. The unit of currency is the Cyprus Pound CY£ and is divided into 100 cents (previously 1000 mils). New coins have been introduced which are: ½ cent (5 mils), 1 cent (10 mils), 2 cents (20 mils), 5 cents (50 mils), 10 cents (100 mils), and 20 cents. Those in brackets are the corresponding old values.

Bank notes remain the same and will be gradually replaced by the new values. They are (500 mils) new 50 cents, CY£1 and the new CY£5 and CY£10. New CY£20 notes are planned and due out shortly.

The main banking business and dealings are done by the Central Bank of Cyprus which will give advice on any monetary enquiries which you may have: Central Bank of Cyprus, 36 Metochiou Street, P.O. Box 1087, Nicosia, Tel 445281.

All your banking business and exchange of money can be done in one of the following banks which have main offices in Paphos (Ktima) main shopping area and also have smaller branches at Kato Paphos and Polis.

They are: **Bank of Cyprus; Popular Bank (Laiki); Hellenic Bank; Co-Operative Bank; Barclays Bank; National Bank of Greece; Lombard Bank.**

Banks open daily Mon-Sat 8.30am to 12 noon. Exchange of travellers cheques can be done by hotels and large shops. You may bring in as much foreign currency as you want but on departing you are not allowed to take any currency over a certain sum which at present is about £40, although unchanged travellers cheques are no problem, so do not exchange more of your travellers cheques than is necessary.

The two main Cyprus banks have head offices and branches in London:
Bank of Cyprus (London) Ltd.
27-31 Charlotte Street,
London W1P 4BH.
Cyprus Popular Bank: 23 Fitzroy Street, London W1P 6BA.

- We welcome any views, ideas and general information which will enable us to improve this publication.
- We also welcome your personal experiences during your stay in Paphos. Please send anything to us now.

OTHER INFORMATION

PUBLIC HOLIDAYS

Some of the holidays are observed Nationally, others by educational or civil service or by the public.

January: 1st-New Year; 6th-Epiphane; 19th-Name day of Archbishop Makarios.

Good Friday/Easter Saturday-Sunday-Monday

March 25th-Greek National Day.

April 1st-Cyprus National Day.

May 1st-Labour Day.

August 3rd-Anniversary of Death of Archbishop Makarios.

October 1st-Independence Day; 28th-Greek National Day.

December 24th, 25th, 26th, — CHRISTMAS.

OPENING HOURS OF PUBLIC PLACES

Opening hours vary according to the season and you may get up-to-date times from the Tourist Office. Museums and archaeological sites usually open: Mon-Fri 7.30am-5.00pm; Sat. 7.30am-5.00pm; Sun. 10.00am-1.00pm (museum only).

Some places close for one or two hours for lunch. Winter times are shorter.

MONASTERIES

These Monasteries have been described in the excursions section and they are: Ayios Neophytos and Khrysorroyiatissa. Please note the following.

● Accommodation is offered in both for a limited number of nights.

● A small donation to the Church is always welcome.

● The monasteries are included in organised tours.

● Visitors, especially women are advised to avoid wearing short trousers and to be dressed decently.

● During Sundays and after the morning service, Christenings usually take place and visitors are welcome to watch.

● Paniyiri (Religious fairs) take place: at Ayios Neophitos:—Jan. 23-24 and Sept. 27-28 at Khrysorroyiatissa: Feb 1-2 and August 14-15.

ENGLISH LANGUAGE NEWSPAPERS

There is a daily English language paper called **"Cyprus Mail"** and a much larger weekly called **"Cyprus Weekly"** both providing local, British and International news, local radio and TV programmes, festivals, events, sports, art and eating places. National British newspapers can also be found at certain places one day later.

RADIO AND TELEVISION

The Cyprus Broadcasting Corporation provides daily radio and television services in Greek, with special programmes in Turkish, English, Armenian and French. Special tourist broadcasts are made during the summer time mainly in English, German and French. For times please consult your hotel or look into the Cyprus Mail or Cyprus Weekly for details.

Do not be surprised if you tune into an English language radio station: this is the BFBS (British Forces Broadcasting Service — Cyprus) and broadcasts in English daily on medium wave and VHF.

Details of daily programmes can be found in the Cyprus Mail.

DIPLOMATIC MISSIONS

All Diplomatic Missions are based in Nicosia, the capital of the island. They include:

UK HIGH COMMISSION - Alexander Pallis St. (02) 473131

FRENCH EMBASSY - 6 Ploutarchos St. Engomi (02) 465258/463687

GERMAN EMBASSY - 10 Nikitaras St. (02) 444362/444037

GREEK EMBASSY - 8-10 Byron Avenue (02) 441880

ITALIAN EMBASSY - 15 Themistodeous St. (02) 473183/4

U.S.A. EMBASSY - Theorissou St. (02) 465151

UNFCYP - Headquarters (02) 464000

AUSTRALIA - 4 Annis Komninis Street (02) 473001

PLEASE REMEMBER . . .

Antiquities are important to Cyprus' culture. Therefore it is absolutely forbidden to export any kind of archaeological items, whether large or small, without proper permission obtained from the Director of the Department of Antiquities in Nicosia.

It is also illegal to remove any antiquities or stones from archaeological sites or the sea bed.

PAPHOS, A PLACE TO RETIRE

Paphos, from all other places in the island, is the most popular place to retire and settle. The place has already attracted a large number of people, mainly British who have settled and bought their own home or apartment either by the sea, around Coral Bay or in the villages above Paphos with their commanding panoramic views.

Others have bought a holiday home which they use for their holidays and also rent it out to other tourists.

Paphos has been chosen as an ideal place for retirement due to the mild climate, the beautiful landscapes, variety of excellent and inexpensive food, wines and brandies and the traditional friendliness and hospitality of its people.

The British community now amounts to a considerable number and they have formed their own association.

For those wishing to purchase a flat or a house or to make Paphos as their permanent place of residence, contact one of the specialist developers who will arrange it for you or the Cyprus Tourism Organisation who will advise you where to apply.

PUBLIC BUILDINGS & SERVICES ▬▬▬

POST OFFICE. The main office providing all postal services including new issues for stamp collectors is situated at Nikodimou Milona St. Opening hours Mon-Fri, 7.30am-1.30pm and 3.30pm-5.30pm. Early closing Wed. Sat 7.30am-12.30pm.

Just recently the main offices have moved to Pano Pervolia at Eleftherios Venizelos Ave.

Post office boxes can be obtained. Other small branches exist in other parts of the town, at Polis and some major villages.

POLICE STATION. This is situated in Kennedy Square and close to 28th October Square. It is the headquarters of the Paphos district and its buildings resemble old colonial architecture. Officers will be glad to assist you with any problems you may have. Call 199 for emergencies or 240140 for general information.

GENERAL HOSPITAL. This is situated at Anavargos village, north of Pano Pervolia (Tel. 240111/2) and is part of Cyprus' Free Medical Care. Visitors to Paphos can visit the hospital should they have any problems (see also under Medical Care).

TOWN HALL. Situated to the east of 28th October Square where events and exhibitions take place at certain times.

TELEGRAPHIC OFFICE/ TELECOMMUNICA-TIONS. Situated at Georgious Griva Dhigeni Ave and can connect you with any part of the world. Direct TELEPHONE connections exist with many countries. Most operators speak English and will help with any enquiries. Dial 192. The telephone directory is printed in both Greek and English.

To dial direct: Athens-00301, London-00441, Paris-00331, Bonn-00492228, New York-001212, Rome-00396.

Inland Dial codes: **Paphos-(06)** (from outside Paphos), Nicosia-(02); Limassol-(05); Larnaca-(04); Ayia Napa (03); Paralimni (03).

PUBLIC LIBRARY. Situated to the west of 28th October Square. This small library has a considerable number of books in Greek but also in English and a few in French. Lending facilities are available. Another library also operates on a lending basis, that of the Anglo-American school (22-26 Hellas Ave). Opening hours: Tue & Fri 10.00am-12.30/ 2.30pm-4.30pm, Wed 2.30pm - 4.30pm.

THE SCHOOLS. These buildings are in Grecian style to the north of 28th October Square and George Grivas Dhigenis Ave and house an elementary school, an economics higher education school and the Gymnasium where in its large hall, concerts, plays and lectures take place. Behind is the old stadium where track field activities and football take place except during the summer days when it's too hot.

COURTS/DISTRICT ADMINISTRATION. These buildings are situated at Nicodimou Milonas St. close to the general post office and are of British colonial architectural style.

USEFUL TELEPHONES
Paphos Code (06)

Town Hall & Services	232116
District Court	2400245
Agricultural Dept.	240260
Fisheries Department	240268
Handicraft Shop	240243
District Governor	240200
Police Headquarters	240140
Harbour Police	240154
Fire Service	240160
Customs Office	240293
Central Post Office	240223
District Archaeological Dept. & Museum	240215
General Hospital	240111
Cyprus Airways	233556
Paphos Airport	240171
Airport Customs	240192

OTHER INTERWORLD PUBLICATIONS ON CYPRUS

(1) **THE MAKING OF MODERN CYPRUS** — Dr. S. Panteli — 286 Pages — 150 illustrations

(2) **THE TASTE OF CYPRUS** — A seasonal look at Cypriot Cooking — Gilli Davies 208 pages — Many colour & b/w illustrations

(3) **APHRODITE CYPRIS** — The Mythology of Cyprus Stass Paraskos — 128 pages — illustrated

(4) **GOOD FOOD GUIDE** to Cyprus in association with the Consumers Association

(5) **EXPLORE CYPRUS** — A tourist Guide — R. Lavithis 208 pages — 140 colour photos — many maps & plans

(6) **CYPRUS IN PICTURES** Full colour pictorial book — 144 pages — 330 pictures — **Sold out** — new edition due in 1993 —

(7) **THE FLORAL CHARM OF CYPRUS** — Valerie Sinclair 208 pages — 188 colour plates

ACCOMMODATION

Accommodation in Paphos caters for all pockets and all requirements. All officially rated accommodation by the Cyprus Tourism Organisation is listed here.

Some hotels in Paphos are excellent, luxurious, with top service, competing with the best in the world. They are expensive but worth every penny. However, the service varies from one to the other.

Quality self catering apartments are also very popular.

Other accommodation such as tourist apartment complexes, villas and special houses can be viewed in some specialist holiday brochures or booked direct. These are not listed here.

There are private individuals who let their houses or apartments in estate complexes. This is arranged through development companies who act as agents, also tourist agencies, but you should take care since overcharging or poor accommodation could create problems.

Monasteries; provide overnight or short stay accommodation without charge, a voluntary contribution towards the monastery is advisable.

During the busy summer months it is better to check for availability due to the large number of tourists. Accommodation also is provided at **Stavros tis Psokas** forest station. Please contact the Forestry Office at Nicosia.

CAMPING

There is a well organised camping site between Polis and the sea, close to the beach. There are toilets, showers, cooking and washing facilities, cafeteria and supermarket. Contact **POLIS Camping** — Polis tel (06) 321526 for information.

Other camping sites are **Feggari** at the Coral Bay area tel. 621534 and Zeno Gardens at Yeroskipou area tel. 233192.

YOUTH HOSTELS

Paphos has a youth hostel which is situated to the north east part of the town and offers accommodation mainly to members of the **International Youth Hostels Association.** The address is 37 Eleftherios Venizelos Avenue, Paphos tel. 221588 or 232588.

At Stavros tis Psokas, in the centre of Paphos forest, there is a small hostel with 12 beds.

For both hostels contact:
Cyprus Youth Hostels Assoc. P.O. Box 1328 — Nicosia.

ALL HOTELS & APARTMENTS

- Provide laundry and dry-cleaning facilities, mainly contracted to an outside company and you pay accordingly.
- All have shops providing essential items, souvenirs, books, some have hairdressing and other facilities. Apartments supply basic provisions for cooking.
- Many establishments provide evening entertainment.
- You are free to go to any establishment to drink at the bar or the cafeteria, eat at the restaurant or enquire about their special evenings.

A complete list of all Hotels and Self Catering apartments is produced annually by the Cyprus Tourism Organisation and can be obtained free, on request.

ROCHESTER
MEDICAL CENTRE

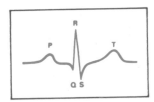

IN-PATIENTS

The Centre is fully equipped to look after fourteen acute and twelve longterm in-patients.
Facilities include:

- A high-density coronary care unit designed to provide round-the-clock intensive therapy and nursing care.
- An out-patients department to deal with emergencies, traumatology and minor operations.
- A modern operating theatre using the most up-to-date equipment.
- Radiology
- Laboratory
- Cardio-diagnostic unit for the early detection of coronary heart disease.

OUT-PATIENTS

Apart from **General Medicine** and **General Surgery,** consultants will be available for the following:

- Cardiology
- Dermatology
- Gastroenterology
- Endocrinology
- Diabetes and Metabolic Deseases
- Paediatrics
- Vascular Surgery
- Cosmetic Surgery

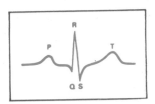

Physicians and surgeons are of the highest standard and qualifications, fully registered and qualified in the U.K. The nursing staff consists of trained and nurses-in-traning from the Royal College of Nursing in England.

TOMBS OF KINGS ROAD
P.O.BOX 302
PAPHOS-CYPRUS
Tel: (06) 234853/ /246960
Fax: (06) 233966

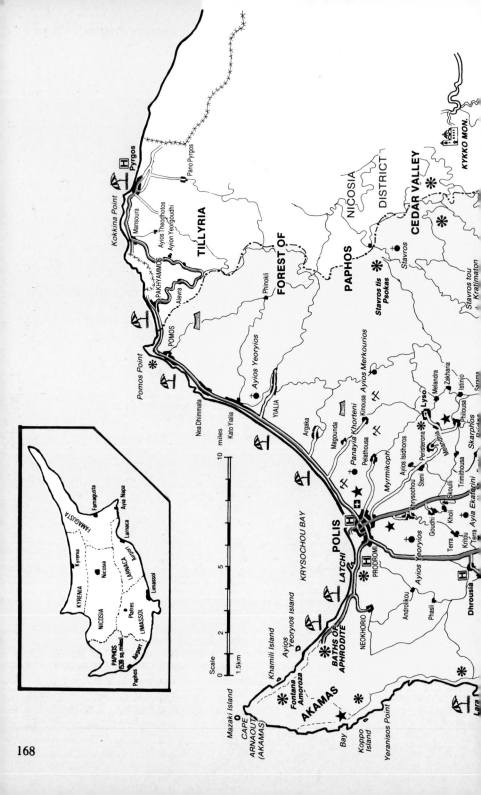

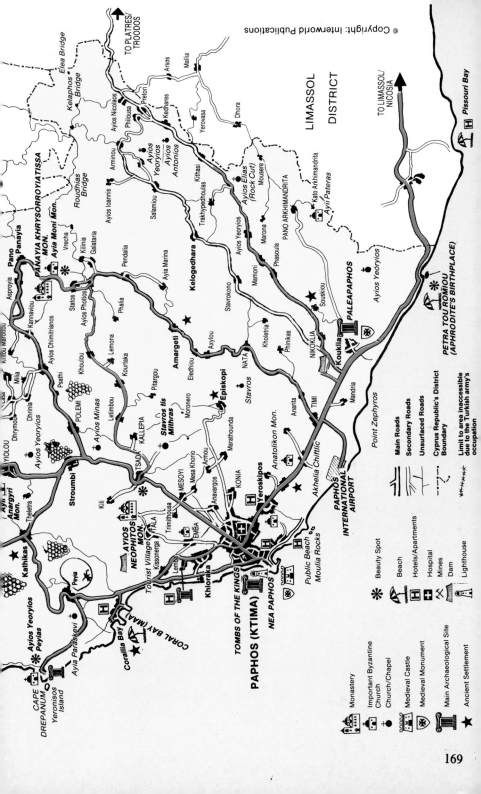

TO PLATRES/
TROODOS

Elea Bridge
Kelaphos Bridge
Kilou Marottou
Roudhias Bridge
Ayios Nicolaos
Philousa
Arsos
Malia
Pretori
Kedhares
Yerovasa
Aminou
Dhora

PANAYIA KHRYSORROYIATISSA MON.
Ayia Moni Mon.
Pano Panayia
Asproyia
Kannaviou
Vrecha
Statos
Ayios Photios
Kilinia
Galataria
Ayios Ioannis
Salamiou
Ayios Yeoryios
Ayios Antonios
Kithasi
Trakhypedhoulas
Ayios Elias (Rock Cut)
Mousere

LIMASSOL
DISTRICT

TO LIMASSOL/
NICOSIA

Pano
Panayia
Ayios Dhimitrianos
Psathi
Dhrinia
Milia
Pendalia
Phalia
Ayia Marina
Stavrokono
Ayios Yeoryios
Marona
Pano Arkhimandrita
Kato Arkhimandrita
Ayii Pateras

Pissouri Bay

Kelogedhara
Khoulou
Lemona
Kourtaka
Letimbou
Pitargou
Axylou
Eledhiou
Mamoni
Phasoula
Souskiou
Ayios Yeoryios

PALEAPAPHOS

PETRA TOU ROMIOU
(APHRODITE'S BIRTHPLACE)

POLEMI
Ayios Minas
Stroumbi
Kili
TSADA
KALLEPIA
Moronero
Marathounda
Amou
Mesa Khorio
Amargeti
Episkopi
Stavros tis Mithras
Stavros
NATA
Kholetria
Phinikas
Anarita
NIKOKLIA
Koukila
Limit to area inaccessible
due to the Turkish army's occupation

YIOLOU
Dhrymou
Ayios Yeoryios
Theletra
MESOYI
Trimithousa
EMBA
Anavargos
KONIA
Yeroskipos
Akhelia Chiftlic
Anatolikon Mon.
TIMI
Mandria
Point Zephyros

Ayia Anargyri Mon.
Kathikas
Peyia
Tourist Village
Kissonerga
Kloraka
Lemba
YALA
AYIOS NEOPHITOS MON.
TOMBS OF THE KINGS
NEA PAPHOS
PAPHOS (KTIMA)
Public Beach
Moulia Rocks
PAPHOS INTERNATIONAL AIRPORT

Ayios Yeoryios Peyias
CAPE DREPANUM
Yeronisos Island
Ayia Paraskevi
CORAL BAY (MAA)
Coralia Bay

Main Roads
Secondary Roads
Unsurfaced Roads
Cyprus Republic's District Boundary
Limit to area inaccessible due to the Turkish army's occupation

Beauty Spot
Beach
Hotels/Apartments
Hospital
Mines
Dam
Lighthouse

Monastery
Important Byzantine Church
Church/Chapel
Medieval Castle
Medieval Monument
Main Archaeological Site
Ancient Settlement

WE CARE FOR OUR GUESTS

At Popular Bank you get Cypriot hospitality at its best - because we see you as our guest.

You can get your money changed at competitive rates, with speed and convenience, from any of our 126 branches all over Cyprus, including all tourist areas.

Furthermore, our Automatic Teller Machine network (Autobank), is connected to VISA International, enabling you to withdraw local currency from the account you hold in your country.

We offer quality banking backed by state-of-the-art technology. But we feel that this is not enough.

At Popular Bank we want to treat you like a guest. And in Cyprus we really care for our guests.

FREE BOOKLET

POPULAR BANK HELPS YOU LEARN BASIC GREEK

Ask for our "Welcome to Cyprus" booklet which can be obtained free of charge at any of our branches. Publications on the Cyprus economy are also available free of charge.

POPULAR BANK

WE CARE FOR YOU

In Association with HongkongBank

Savvas Pottery

Studio   Shop
KOLONI — PAPHOS
Tel: (06) 234804   Fax: (06) 245636

★ **Traditional Shapes & Designs**

★ **Copies from the Museum**

★ **Kitchenware (Leadfree Glazes)**

★ **Decorative articles, vases bowls etc.**

★ **Personal orders are accepted — Delivery within 5 to 10 days.**

where to find the Famous Savvas Pottery

SAVVAS POTTERY
SUPPLIES A GREAT NUMBER OF SHOPS, HOTELS
AND RESTAURANTS ALL OVER THE ISLAND

Acclaimed for its fine Italian cuisine, excellent service and relaxing atmosphere.

Reservations: 09-516345

Cavallini
Ristorante Italiano